A Guide to Foreign Missionary Manuscripts in the Presbyterian Historical Society

Frederick J. Heuser, Jr.

A Publication of
The Presbyterian Historical Society

Bibliographies and Indexes in World History,
Number 11

Greenwood Press
New York • Westport, Connecticut • London

Library of Congress Cataloging-in-Publication Data

Presbyterian Historical Society.
    A guide to foreign missionary manuscripts in the Presbyterian
Historical Society / Frederick J. Heuser, Jr.
    p.   cm. — (A Publication of the Presbyterian Historical
Society) (Bibliographies and indexes in world history, ISSN
0742-6852 ; no. 11)
    Includes index.
    ISBN 0-313-26249-7 (lib. bdg. : alk. paper)
    1. Presbyterian Church—Missions—Manuscripts—Catalogs.
2. Presbyterian Church—Missions—History—Sources—Bibliography—
Catalogs.   3. Manuscripts, American—Pennsylvania—Philadelphia—
Catalogs.   4. Presbyterian Historical Society—Archives—Catalogs.
I. Heuser, Frederick J.   II. Title.   III. Series.   IV. Series:
Contributions to the study of religion. Publication of the
Presbyterian Historical Society.
Z6611.M65P73 1988
[BV2570]
016.266'5—dc 19   87-34088

British Library Cataloguing in Publication Data is available.

Copyright © 1988 by The Presbyterian Historical Society

Library of Congress Catalog Card Number: 87-34088
ISBN: 0-313-26249-7
ISSN: 0742-6852

First published in 1988

Greenwood Press, Inc.
88 Post Road West, Westport, Connecticut 06881

Printed in the United States of America

The paper used in this book complies with the
Permanent Paper Standard issued by the National
Information Standards Organization (Z39.48-1984).

10 9 8 7 6 5 4 3 2 1

Contents

vi Contents

Illustrations

The photographs are from the files of the
Presbyterian Historical Society. The maps were
taken from the Board of Foreign Missions'<u>Centennial</u>
<u>Series</u> and the denomination's <u>Yearbook</u> <u>of</u> <u>Prayer</u>.

Maps

Abbreviations

ABCFM	American Board of Commis- for Foreign Missions
ARPC	Associate Reformed Presbyte- rian Church
APC	Associate Presbyterian Church
BFM	Board of Foreign Missions
CMUSA	Calvinistic Methodist Church in the U.S.A.
COEMAR	Commission on Ecumenical Mis- sions and Relations
CPC	Cumberland Presbyterian Church
FOL	Folder (s)
MF	Microfilm
N.S.	New School
O.S.	Old School
PCUS	Presbyterian Church in the U.S. (1865-1983)
PCUSA	Presbyterian Church in the U.S.A. (1789-1958)

PC (U.S.A.)   Presbyterian Church (U.S.A.)
                       (1983 -)

R   Reel (s)

RG   Record Group

UPCNA   United Presbyterian Church of
                       North America (1858-1958)

UPCUSA   United Presbyterian Church in
                       the U.S.A. (1958-1983)

V   Volume (s)

Preface

This guide is intended to provide an overview of the foreign missionary manuscripts and archival collections of the Presbyterian Historical Society. It includes all collections acquired and processed through January 1, 1987. The planned second edition will include materials acquired and processed after that date.

I wish to thank my colleagues at the Presbyterian Historical Society for their encouragement, support, and patience, without which the creation of this guide would have been impossible. Special thanks, however, are due to William B. Miller, director of the Presbyterian Historical Society, for his initial and continued support throughout what seemed at times a never-ending project. Special thanks are also in order to the Reverend Oscar J. McCloud and the Program Agency of the Presbyterian Church (U.S.A.) for their assistance in helping to fund this project.

A number of individuals read the manuscript and rendered valuable suggestions and insights. My gratitude for this help is extended to Robert Benedetto, Gerald W. Gillette, Barbara J. MacHaffie, John M. Mulder, James Smylie and Gordon Tait. Gerald Gillette's keen editorial skills were tested more than he or I probably ever anticipated. This guide is a better product because of those skills. The staff of the archives department likewise made the job of completing this project easier and deserves special thanks. Janet Bishop made valuable recommendations and offered continued moral support during the last two years of the project, as did her successor, Kristin L. Gleeson. Special thanks are also extended to Cynthia Harris and Linda Grzywacz at Greenwood Press for their patience, understanding, and assistance throughout this project.

Most of all, I am grateful for the support and encouragement of Lorraine Baggett-Heuser, who humored me with her wit, tolerated my incessant ramblings about missionaries, and had the difficult task of living with me and this project for the last four years. For her patience, interest, and understanding I am indebted.

Research at the
Presbyterian Historical Society

When the Presbyterian Historical Society was
established in 1852, the founders stated that their
objective "was to collect and preserve materials of
the history of the Presbyterian Church in the United
States of America and to promote the knowledge of
said history as far as possible."1 From its beginnings in 1852 until the present, Philadelphia, where
the first presbytery was established in 1708, has
been the Society's home. From 1898 until 1967 the
Society was located in the Witherspoon building at
Broad and Juniper streets, at which time it moved to
its new location at 425 Lombard Street, in the heart
of the city's historic district.

In 1923, the Society was designated as the
Department of History of the Office of the General
Assembly, thus making it an official agency of the
Presbyterian Church in the United States of America.
Following the 1983 reunion between the United Presbyterian Church in the United States of America and
the Presbyterian Church in the United States, the
Society shared with the Historical Foundation in
Montreat, North Carolina, the responsibility for
preserving and documenting the work of the Presbyterian Church (U.S.A.). In 1987, the Society was
designated as the Office of History of the Presbyterian Church (U.S.A.), and since January 1, 1988
has served as the national archives for the new denomination.

Since its origins, the Society has gathered
materials related to American Presbyterian life and
made them available to all who might be interested.

The Society's library contains printed materials
about history and Christianity in general from the
fifteenth century to the present. Also included are
extensive collections of non-print media pertinent
to American Presbyterian and Reformed church life,
including engravings, photographs, lantern and 35 mm
slides, microfilm, motion picture film, filmstrips,
phono discs, audiotapes, and museum items. The Society established its formal archival program in
1967. This guide presents evidence of the accom-
plishments of that program's first two decades and
reflects the denominational diversity in the Presbyterian Church (U.S.A.)'s background which in 1987
celebrated the 150th anniversary of the founding of
the Board of Foreign Missions.

    Besides serving as the national archives for
the Presbyterian Church (U.S.A.), the Society also
serves as the archives for other ecumenical organizations in which Presbyterians have been involved.
These include the National Council of Churches of
Christ, the American Sunday School Union, the American Foreign Christian Union, and the National Temperance Society. The Society's archives contains
official minutes and files of General Assemblies,
presbyteries, synods, and individual congregations
of diverse American and Reformed denominations.
Also included are records of foreign and domestic
missions, women's work in the church and society,
and immigrant and ethnic minority work. The Sheldon
Jackson Collection documents the history of the
American West and Alaska. Personal papers from individuals such as Albert Barnes, John Wilbur Chap-
man, Henry van Dyke, Eugene Carson Blake, Donald
Barnhouse, and Margaret Kuhn are also held in the
archives.

    The Society is open to the public Monday
through Friday from 8:30 a.m. until 4:30 p.m., and
is closed on weekends and legal holidays. Information concerning use of its collections can either be
obtained in person or by writing to the Society.
Generally, archival records less than seventy-five-
years-old require special permission before access
can be granted. Official records less than twenty-
five-years old are unavailable for public use. Information regarding access to a particular collection can be obtained by contacting the Society's
archivist. Permission to quote for publication must
be obtained from either the Society's director or
the archivist.

Reproduction facilities are available at the Society. Materials designated as "Restricted" may not be photoduplicated in any manner. Information concerning the duplication of materials can be obtained by writing to the Society. The Society's staff collects materials, prepares them for use, and makes them accessible to researchers. Because staff efforts must be balanced in these areas of responsibility, limitations must be placed on the amount of staff time that can be expended on reference inquiries.

Use of this Guide

A repository level guide is defined by what it excludes as well as what it includes. The purpose of this guide is limited to manuscript/archival collections alone that document foreign, that is outside of the continental United States, missionary work. Published materials, of which the Society has extensive holdings, photographic and oral history collections, and museum items fall outside of the scope of this effort.

This guide includes institutional records from the Board of Foreign Missions of the Presbyterian Church in the U.S.A; the United Presbyterian Church of North America and its predecessors; the Cumberland Presbyterian Church; the Calvinistic Methodist Church in the U.S.A; and the Commission on Ecumenical Missions and Relations of the United Presbyterian Church in the U.S.A; as well as personal papers of former Presbyterian missionaries. It does not include home missions that were under the auspices of the Board of National Missions or its predecessors. The contents of the guide are arranged by geographic area. The following information is provided for each entry: title/inclusive dates; size; and access number for arranged archival collections. Known biographical data for personal papers and administrative histories for institutional records are also included. A statement on the collection's arrangement was also included when appropriate.

Missionary materials in general have great research appeal to a variety of scholars. Denomina-

tional scholars have long realized their value in
documenting the church's work at home and abroad.
Scholars interested in developing Third World countries have also recognized their importance, as have
students of diplomatic history. More recently, however, students of American social history have dis-
covered their value in documenting the role of women
and ethnic minorities in the United States as well
as other diverse subjects.

Though the Presbyterian Historical Society has
extensive missionary material holdings, researchers
should be aware of some of the other institutions
that contain Presbyterian missionary materials. The
missionary records of the former Presbyterian Church
in the United States can be found in Montreat, North
Carolina. Records of the Cumberland Presbyterian
Church are located at the Society as well as in
Nashville, Tennessee. The records of the Yale China
Project and the American Board of Commissioners for
Foreign Missions, though not exclusively Presbyterian, can be located at Yale and Harvard universities respectively. Records of missions transferred from the ABCFM to the PCUSA are held in part in
the Society's archives.

Some personal papers of Presbyterian missionaries can be found in the Universities of Oregon,
Virginia, Michigan, Lincoln University, the University of Tulsa, and Mt. Holyoke College. In cooperation with the Presbyterian Library Association,
the Society maintains the Union List Of Presbyterian
Manuscripts -- a guide to such resources held in li-
braries across the country. Students and scholars
are also urged to check the National Union Catalog
of Manuscript Collections. Other institutions pos-
sessing Presbyterian missionary records are encouraged to inform the Society of their holdings.

Presbyterians In Mission:
An Historic Overview

The establishment in 1837 of the Presbyterian
Church in the U.S.A.'s (O.S.) Board of Foreign Missions signaled the beginning of a worldwide mission-
nary operation destined to embrace approximately
fifteen countries located on four different conti-
nents. Presbyterian interest in foreign missions
however predated the creation of the BFM by almost
three-quarters of a century.

The American Presbyterian church has been com-
mitted from its inception to the belief that it is a
missionary church and that every member is a missionary. By the end of the eighteenth century, increasing interest in missions was manifested by the
creation of several local and independent missionary
societies including the New York Missionary Society
(1796); the Northern Berkshire and Columbia Mission-
nary Societies (1797); the Missionary Society of
Connecticut (1798); the Massachusetts Missionary Society (1799); and the Boston Female Society for Missionary Purposes (1800). These societies helped to
prepare the foundation for the later and larger denominational boards. Though membership was interdenominational, Presbyterians were prominent in several, notably the New York and Northern societies.
societies.2

While many individual Presbyterians were active in these missionary societies, the church's
judicatories were not indifferent to the subject of
missions. As early as 1763, the Synod of New York
ordered that a collection for missions be taken,
with a pronouncement in 1767 that this be done an-

nually. At the first General Assembly in 1789, each
of the four synods were requested to recommend two
missionaries to the General Assembly the following
year, whose support was to be provided by the presbyteries. In 1802, the General Assembly created a
Standing Committee on Missions that theoretically
worked in conjunction with the presbyteries and
European missionary societies. Successive General
Assemblies authorized additional funds and in a
single year the Standing Committee on Missions
reported the appointment of fifty-one new missionaries. In 1816, the Standing Committee recommended
to the General Assembly that it be merged into a
more permanent organization known as the "Board of
Missions acting under the authorization of the
General Assembly of the Presbyterian Church in the
U.S.A." The General Assembly authorized and directed the Board to establish church auxiliary missionary societies that would extend its own operation.3

In 1817, the General Assembly joined the Dutch
Reformed and Associate Reformed Churches in estab-
lishing the United Foreign Missionary Society. The
Society's constitution declared that "the object of
the Society shall be to spread the Gospel among the
Indians of North America, the inhabitants of Mexico
and South America, and in other portions of the
heathen and anti-Christian world."4 In 1826, the
Society's work was transferred to the Congregational
Church's American Board of Commissioners for Foreign
Missions primarily because it was felt that the
existence of two missionary organizations appealing
to the same constituency was unwise and that a merger would strengthen the expanding operations of the
ABCFM. Hence, the ABCFM became the recognized missionary agency for both the Congregationalist and
Presbyterian churches.5

Despite the transfer of Presbyterian work to
the ABCFM, many Presbyterians believed that a denominational mission board was preferable to an
independent association of Christians like the
ABCFM. The General Assembly remained nominally com-
mitted to the latter. In 1831, when it became evident that the General Assembly was not prepared to
establish a denominational board, the Synod of
Pittsburgh did so by organizing the Western Foreign
Missionary Society. In 1837, those forces that had
been advocating a denominational board finally pre-
vailed when the work of the Western Foreign Missionary Society, upon recommendation of the General
Assembly (O.S.), was transferred to the PCUSA's

newly formed Board of Foreign Missions.6

The creation of the Board of Foreign Missions thus marked the culmination of a controversy whether missionary operations should be implemented by voluntary societies or by the church in its organized capacity. All Presbyterians were not in agreement over its formation however. As part of the broader conflict between Old/New School Presbyterians, New School adherents opposed the Board's formation and continued to support the ABCFM until the two factions were reunited in 1870.

The PCUSA's Board of Foreign Missions was organized to convey the gospel "to whatever parts of the heathen and anti-Christian world the Providence of God might enable the Society to extend its evangelical exertions."7 Throughout much of the nineteenth century, the BFM directed the church's foreign as well as some domestic missionary activities. Before 1870, foreign missions were established in Africa, Brazil, China, Colombia, India, Japan, and Thailand. Following the reunion of the Old/New School denominations in 1870, the BFM absorbed the ABCFM's mission work in Iran, Iraq, and Syria and expanded its own operation by initiating new work in Korea, Central and South America, and the Philippines. Missions to the native American, Jewish, and Oriental populations throughout the United States, which had begun under the BFM, were subsequently transferred to the Board of Home Missions in 1885, 1894, and 1922 respectively.8

While the PCUSA was developing missions throughout much of the nineteenth and early twentieth centuries, other Presbyterian denominations were also active in this area. The Board of Missions of the Cumberland Presbyterian Church commenced its foreign mission work in 1852, though earlier efforts evidence this church's work with native Americans. The Associate Presbyterian Church initiated missionary work in Trinidad in 1842 but was forced after considerable difficulty there to turn its work over to the Free Church of Scotland a decade later. The APC's work in India began in 1852. The Associate Reformed Presbyterian Church began its work in Syria in 1844 and in Egypt in 1853. In 1858, the APC and the APRC merged to form the United Presbyterian Church of North America. The mission work in India, Syria, and Egypt started by these denominations was subsequently transferred to the UPCNA and placed under the auspices of its

newly formed Board of Foreign Missions. UPCNA
mission work would later extend to China, the Sudan,
and Abyssinia. Following the merger of the PCUSA
and the UPCNA in 1958, the mission work in India,
the Sudan, and Ethiopia (Abyssinia) were transferred
to the UPCUSA. With the establishment of the PCUS
at the end of the Civil War in 1865, missionary work
was eventually initiated in China, Korea, Japan,
Mexico, and throughout Latin America.

The Presbyterian Church in the U.S.A.'s foreign missionary enterprise in the nineteenth century
was responsible for the establishment of indigenous
churches, a variety of educational facilities, hospitals, orphanages, seminaries, and other institutions that reflected the church's educational, medical and evangelical ministry. The church's missionary operation continued to expand throughout the
twentieth century, changing in response to forces
both within and outside of the church. Tumultuous
events of this century -- world war, civil war, and
the emergence of Third World nationalism -- have
altered both the scope and direction of foreign missionary work. These events, for all intents and
purposes, resulted in an end to the political, economic, and religious forms of colonialism as prac-
ticed by the West, though vestiges of these are
still powerful irritants in different areas.

Many of the churches established by missionary
activity in the nineteenth century achieved maturity
by the twentieth century and were ready to assume
responsibility for the mission of the church. A
deep awareness of the implications of these changes
was articulated in the 1956 Lake Monhonk Conference
in New York. Following the merger of the PCUSA and
the UPCNA in 1958 a new organization, the Commission
on Ecumenical Mission and Relations, was formed to
reflect the "new day" of twentieth century mis-
sions.9

COEMAR continued the policy of encouraging the
growth of indigenous churches in each country where
it had responsibilities. That is, churches that
could be completely at home in the culture of that
country and simultaneously free from control by any
other agency. COEMAR also sought to foster a national leadership with ecumenical, missionary vi-
sion. Until recently, many of the so-called
"younger churches" were handicapped because they
were largely products of Western missions and unable
to develop independently. COEMAR's policy was to

transfer to these national churches the responsibilities that belonged to autonomous bodies.

COEMAR sought to prepare its own missionaries,
now referred to as "fraternal workers," to serve the
national leadership of the indigenous churches and
to engage in new relationships of service. After
1958, the mission as an entity or organization was
either dissolved or "integrated" within the life of
the church in that country. The philosophy under-
lying COEMAR's actions implied a shift in emphasis
from a decision-making missionary agency to churches
across the world as they assumed new responsibility
for decisions that had formerly been made by a Mission board. This philosophy continued following the
church's general reorganization in 1972, with
COEMAR's responsibilities now being absorbed into
the new Program Agency. This attitude, evident as
early as 1956, has since had far-reaching conse-
quences for the development of a world-wide Christian Church.

Endnotes

1. Constitution of the Presbyterian Historical
Society, adopted 20 May 1852.

2. Arthur Judson Brown. One Hundred Years: A
History of the Foreign Missionary Work of the
Presbyterian Church in the U.S.A., With Some
Accounts of Countries, Peoples and the Policies and
Problems of Modern Missions. (New York: Fleming H.
Revell Company, 1936), 14.

3. Ibid., 15.

4. Constitution of the Presbyterian Historical
Society, adopted 20 May 1852.

5. Brown, One Hundred Years, 6.

6. Ibid., 20-21.

7. Constitution of the Presbyterian Historical
Society, adopted 20 May 1852.

8. Brown, One Hundred Years, 22.

9. John Coventry Smith, From Colonialism To World
Community. (Philadelphia: The Geneva Press, 1982),
165-170.

1. Newly appointed and furloughed missionaries and officers of the Board of Foreign Missions, New York City, June 1899.

2. Robert E. Speer, circa 1927. Secretary of the Board of Foreign Missions, 1891-1937.

A Guide to
Foreign Missionary Manuscripts
in the
Presbyterian Historical Society

AFRICA
SHOWING LOCATION OF
OUR MISSION

WEST AFRICA
MISSION

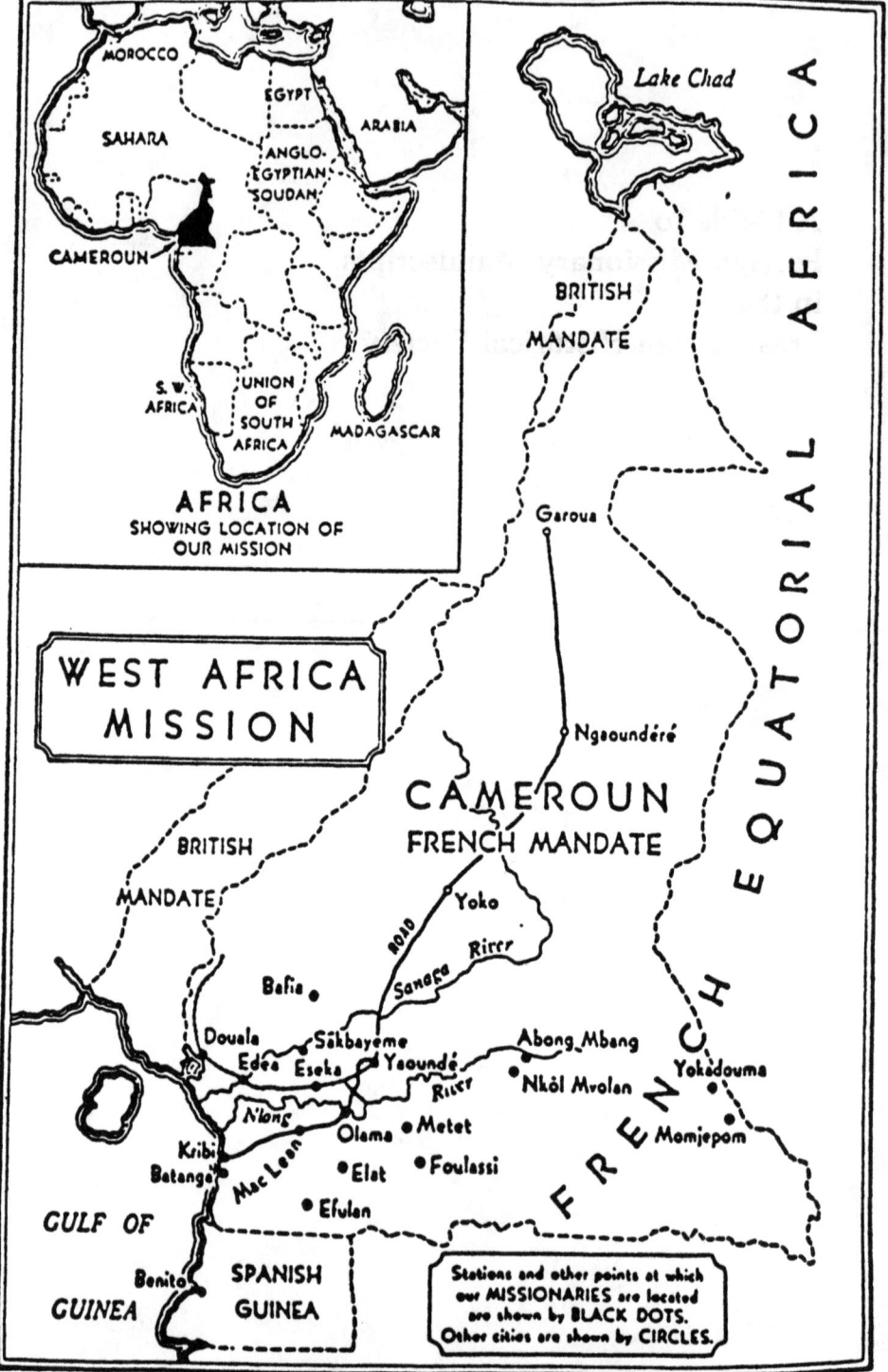

Lake Chad

BRITISH
MANDATE

Garoua

Ngaoundéré

CAMEROUN
FRENCH MANDATE

BRITISH

MANDATE

Yoko

ROAD

Sanaga River

Bafia

Douala
Edéa   Eséka   Séka bayeme   Yaoundé

Abong Mbang

Nyong River

Nkôl Mvolan

Yokadouma

N'long

Olama   Metet

Kribi

Batanga   Mac Lean

Elat   Foulassi

Momjepom

Efulan

FRENCH EQUATORIAL AFRICA

GULF OF

Benito   SPANISH

GUINEA   GUINEA

Stations and other points at which
our MISSIONARIES are located
are shown by BLACK DOTS.
Other cities are shown by CIRCLES.

AFRICA

The missionary work of the PCUSA in Africa was limited originally to the West Coast of Africa and during the 19th century resulted in the founding of several of mission stations within that area. These included Liberia (1833-1884); Spanish Guinea (1865-
1924; 1932-); Gabon (1871-1972); Ogowe (1874-1892);
and Cameroon (1889-1972). Missionary work in Egypt
was initiated by the ARPC and later continued by the
UPCNA. Work in the Sudan and the Upper Nile was
started by the UPCNA and continued by the UPCUSA
following the 1958 merger. Southern Presbyterian
work in Africa began in the Congo in 1890. The
PCUSA's work in Africa was evangelical, educational
and medical in nature. Working in conjunction with
several other denominations, including the PCUS, the
Methodist and Protestant Episcopal churches, as well
as the ABCFM, the PCUSA's Board of Foreign Missions
supported the construction of hospitals, schools,
seminaries and strove toward the establishment of
self-supporting indigenous churches. Though much
of the PCUSA's 19th century work was concentrated in
Liberia, limited success was also achieved in newer
fields such as Corisco, Spanish Guinea and Gabon.
By the end of the 19th century, the PCUSA's emphasis
was on expanding work in the Cameroon and Spanish
Guinea.

The 20th century work of the PCUSA in both of
these areas was subject to disruption and change
from the effects of world war, economic disloca-
tion and emerging nationalism. Following the end
of the First World War and the subsequent transfer
of Cameroon to France, Presbyterian mission work

expanded into the interior, resulting in the growth
of remote mission stations with the general support
of French colonial officials. This growth, albeit
slow in nature, continued during the late 1940s. In
1957, the Presbyterian Church in the Cameroon became
independent with the formation of its own General
Assembly.

The work of the PCUSA in Spanish Guinea faltered
during the interwar period. The advent of government restrictions and economic difficulties completely halted work there in 1924, though it resumed
again in 1932. In 1958, the Presbytery of Spanish
Guinea, previously associated with the Synod of the
Presbyterian Church in the Cameroon, separated from
that body and became affiliated with the Synod of
New Jersey in anticipation of its becoming an independent church. This was officially realized later
that year with the formation of the Church of Corisco and Rio Muni.

* * * * *

1. AIKIN, RUTH (1885-1970), PAPERS, 1916-70, 1.25
    FT., RG 185

Ruth Aikin was appointed by the PCUSA's BFM to the
West Africa Mission in 1916 and remained there until
her retirement in 1950. She served at Lolodorf
(MacLean Memorial Station), Efulan, Metet and Nkol
Mvolan stations where she taught women and children,
directed several girls' schools and performed evangelistic work.

Arrangement: Series I. Correspondence, 1916-1950;
Series I. Diaries, 1923-1949 (incomplete); Series
III. Photographs, 1916-ca.1965; Series IV. Miscel-
lany, 1921-1945.

2. BEANLAND, GAYLE CAROTHERS (1878-1961), PAPERS,
    1911-38, 1 FOL.

Gayle Carothers Beanland was appointed in 1910 to
the PCUSA's West Africa Mission. He performed medical, educational and evangelistic work at Metet, the
Makae country and along the eastern border of the
Cameroon until his retirement in 1948.

Beanland's papers consist of miscellaneous correspondence, reports, and photographs, 1911-1938.

3. BOARD OF FOREIGN MISSIONS (ARC/UPCNA/PCUSA &
    UPCUSA), RECORDS OF THE EGYPT, ETHIOPIA & SUDAN
    MISSIONS, 1850-1966, 5 FT, 37 V., RG 26/150

The work of the UPCNA in Africa was limited to
Egypt, the Sudan and Ethiopia (Abyssinia). Mission
work in Egypt was begun in 1854 by the ARC under the
name of the Egyptian Missionary Association. The
Associations's objective was to preach the Gospel to
all classes of the Arabic-speaking population, to
train native Christian workers, and to establish an
evangelical Christian Church in Egypt. The methods
used were evangelistic, educational and medical in
nature. After 1858, the UPCNA directed the work of
the Mission through a corporation known as the Board
of Foreign Missions which was responsible for all of
the church's philanthropic work outside of the
United States. In 1900, the Egypt Mission expanded
its operation by sending missionaries into the
Sudan, thus commencing the North Sudan and Upper
Nile Missions. By 1920, UPCNA missionaries had
established a mission in Ethiopia, then known as
Abyssinia. In 1935, the Association became known
as the American Mission in Egypt. After 1958,
mission work in Egypt, the Sudan and Ethiopia was
assumed by COEMAR.

The records of the UPCNA's Board of Foreign Missions
consist mainly of documentation from the Egyptian
Missionary Association/American Mission in Egypt.
Included are correspondence, reports, clippings,
newsletters, speeches and miscellaneous items that
reflect the work of the ARC, the UPCNA, the PCUSA
and the UPCUSA, 1850-1966. Also included are the
Association's minutes, 1860-1958 as well as miscellaneous presbytery and station minutes, 1860-1937.
The records of the Ethiopia mission are limited to
the minutes of the Ethiopia Missionary Association,
1924-1958. Records from the Sudan Mission include
minutes of the North Sudan Missionary Association,
1949-1958; the South Sudan Missionary Association,
1949-1958; and the Sudan Missionary Association,
1905-1948.

4. BOARD OF FOREIGN MISSIONS (PCUSA/UPCUSA), RE-
    CORDS OF THE WEST AFRICA MISSION, 1902-66,
    5 FT., RG 74

Presbyterians began moving into the southeastern interior of the Cameroon following its annexation by
Germany in 1887. Formal work commenced there about
1889 when Presbyterian missionaries Rev. and Mrs.

Burgess Brier were assigned to the newly created
Batanga station. Mission stations were later established at Efulan in 1893; Elat in 1895; Lolodorf in
1897; Metet in 1909; and Foulassi in 1916. Sakbayeme was taken over from the Baptist's Basle Mission in 1917. Yaounde was opened in 1922; Nkol
Mvolan in 1928; Bafia and Edea in 1930; Momjepom in
1933; Ilanga in 1940; and Libamba and Ibong in
1947. Prior to 1936, the churches in the West Africa field were organized as the Presbytery of Corisco and attached to the Synod of New Jersey. In
1936, upon action from the General Assembly, the
Presbytery of Corisco was subdivided into three
presbyteries (Corisco, Metet and Sanaga) and organized into a separate synod known as the Synod of the
Cameroon.

Record group 74 contains materials from the PCUSA
and UPCUSA's West Africa Mission, 1902-1966.

Arrangement: Series I. Minutes, 1902-1959; Series
II. Reports, 1919-1960; Series III. Correspondence, 1917-1966.

5. BOARD OF FOREIGN MISSIONS (PCUSA/UPCUSA), SECRE-
    TARIES' FILES OF THE WEST AFRICA MISSION, 1835-
    1965, [MF, 31 R, 1835-1910; 1856-1965, 13 FT.,
    RG 142, 4 V.]

The West Africa Mission Secretaries' Files documents
the PCUSA's and UPCUSA's missionary work in Liberia
Spanish Guinea, Gabon, Ogowe and the Cameroon. The
microfilmed materials consists of outgoing and incoming correspondence, minutes and reports from the
Liberia, Corisco, Gabon and Cameroon Missions, 1835-
1910. Record group 142 mainly covers the period
from 1911-1965 with emphasis on the work in the
Cameroon, though some Spanish Guinea, Gabon and
Corsico materials are also included.

Arrangement of RG 142: Series I. Miscellany, 1914-
1945; Series II. Correspondence, 1911-1951; Series
III. Missionary Correspondence, 1911-1965; Series
IV. Mission Institutions, 1919-1946; Series V.
Reports, 1911-1939; Gabon and Corisco Minutes, 1856-
1902, 4 v.

6. CRISWELL, ANNA B. (1880-1953), PAPERS, 1897-
    1950, 2 FT., RG 184

Anna B. Criswell was appointed as a missionary to
Egypt by the UPCNA in 1904. She served in the

Pressly Memorial Institute in Assuit, where for
twenty-five years she was principal. She retired
from missionary service in 1950.

Arrangement: Series I. Correspondence, 1914-1944;
Series II. Diaries, 1929-1950; Series III. Photographs, ca. 1897-1950; Series IV. Miscellany, 1897-
1950.

7. DAGER FAMILY PAPERS, 1909-16, .25 FT., RG 207

William M. Dager (1869-1917) and Sarah Shaw Dager
(1870-1936) were appointed to the PCUSA's West Africa Mission in 1899. They served at the Gabon and
Corisco Missions until the upheavals of the First
World War necessitated their return to America in
1916. Their scheduled return to Africa the following year was aborted by William Dager's premature
death. Sarah Shaw Dager did not return to Africa
and resigned from missionary work in 1920.

The Dager Family papers include correspondence, personal reports, photographs and miscellaneous items
which reflect their experiences as missionaries in
West Africa 1909-1916.

8. EMERSON, FRANK OWEN (1874-1952), PAPERS, 1902-
    1952, 1 FT., RG 200

Frank Owen Emerson was appointed as a missionary to
West Africa in 1906 by the PCUSA. He served at the
Maclean Memorial, Batanga, Efulan, Elat, Nkol Mvolan
and Momjepom stations where he performed evangelistic work until his retirement in 1946.

Arrangement: Series I. Correspondence, 1924-1952;
Series II. Manuscripts, [n.d.]; Series III. Daybooks, 1915-1951; Series IV. Miscellany, 1906-1952.

9. FINNEY, MINNIEHAHA (1865-1967), PAPERS, 1947-
    1956, 5 FOL.

Minniehaha Finney was appointed to the Egypt Mission
by the UPCNA's Board of Foreign Missions in 1899 and
served there until her retirement in 1942. Until
1915 she was involved in education work for women
and children in Mansoura and Alexandria. In 1915,
she began evangelistic work in Tanta and was instrumental in establishing there a Training School for
Bible Women.

Her papers includes miscellaneous correspondence and

a variety of unpublished and undated manuscripts
dealing with Egyptian life and culture and with her
work as a missionary.

10. GOOD, ADOLPHUS CLEMENS (1856-1894), PAPERS, 1882-1896, .5 FT., RG 169

Adolphus Clemens Good was appointed by the PCUSA's
Board of Foreign Missions to the West Africa Mission
in 1882. Initially assigned to the Baraka Station,
he was transferred to the Ogowe River area in 1884
where he spent the rest of his career. Designated
by the Board to explore the Batanga area in 1892,
Dr. Good journeyed into the unexplored interior on
three occasions. His first two journeys led to the
selection of Efulan as the site of the first interior station. His third journey, during which he
marched some 400 miles, was the most extensive of
the three and resulted in the selection of Ebolewo
as the second interior station. While on a fourth
journey in 1894, Good contracted blackwater fever
and died in Efulan shortly thereafter. In addition
to his efforts as a teacher and evangelist, Good
studied bird and animal life in the Ogowe Valley and
the Cameroon as well as the ethnology and religious
beliefs of various West African tribes. He prepared
a text on Bulu grammar which was published posthu-
mously.

Dr. Good's papers document his African experiences and
reflect various aspects of African life and culture,
notably, the religious beliefs of the Gabwa and the
role of women in Bulu society.

Arrangement: Series I. Journals/miscellaneous
items, 1882-1892; Series II. Correspondence, 1882-
1896.

11. GOOD, ALBERT IRWIN (1884-1975), PAPERS, 1910-1958, .5 FT, RG 179

Albert Irwin Good, son of African missionary Adol-
phus C. Good, was appointed to the PCUSA's West
Africa Mission in 1909 and served there until 1949.
Most of his career was spent at Maclean Memorial
Station, Lolodorf in the Cameroon. He also served
at Efuland and Elat. Dr. Good was engaged in teach-
ing and evangelistic work. He published a number of
Bulu language items, including a Book of Forms for
Ministers; A Bulu Handbook Supplement and Bulu Folk-
tales. He also translated thirty-five books of the
Old Testament into Bulu and edited various Bulu,

Mabea and Banok language hymnals. Deeply interested
in science, Good collected insects and many of which
were donated to the Carnegie, Cleveland and Stanford
University Museums. A Fellow of the Royal Geographic Society, he published articles about African natural history. He served as Vice-Moderator of the
1935 General Assembly and as Stated Clerk for the
Presbytery of Corisco from 1938-1949. He retired
from church service in 1950.

Dr. Good's papers document only his early years in
Africa.

Arrangement: Series I. Diaries, 1910-1912; 1940;
Series II. Photographs, manuscripts and miscellaneous items, 1910-1958.

12. GOOD, LYDIA BELLE WALKER (1856-1924), DIARIES,
    1909-1920, 2 V.

Lydia Belle Walker Good was appointed to the PCUSA's
West Africa Mission in 1876 following a three year
teaching career at Odanah, Wisconsin among the Oji-
bwa Indians. In 1883, she married missionary Adolphus Clemens Good and served in Gabon, West Africa
where she taught and performed evangelistic work.
Shortly before her husband's death in 1894, she returned to the U.S., remaining there for fifteen
years. She returned to Africa in 1909 and served in
the Cameroon until 1921.

This collection contains Good's diaries for the
years 1909-1914 and 1917-1920.

13. HARVEY, WILLIAM (1835-1908), DIARIES, 1865-
    1908, 10 V.

William Harvey was appointed to the UPCNA's Egypt
Mission in 1865. He remained there until his death
on the field in 1908.

This collection consists of Harvey's diaries for the
period 1865-1908.

14. JOHNSON, SILAS FRANKLIN (1865-1936), PAPERS,
    1889-1936, 2 FT., RG 55

Silas Franklin Johnson was appointed as a medical
missionary to the West Africa by the PCUSA in 1894.
He served in the southern Cameroon until 1900 when
his wife's health necessitated their return to the
U.S. Following her death in 1902, Dr. Johnson re-

turned to Africa where he subsequently remarried in
1904. Though his work was primarily that of a physician and surgeon, Dr. Johnson was instrumental in
creating a written language for the Bulu people. He
retired from missionary service in 1935.

Arrangement: Series I. Personal Correspondence (including items from his two wives, Mary Hays Johnson
and Laura Mosher Johnson) and Miscellaneous Items,
1894-1936; Series II. Diaries, 1894-1934.

15. JOHNSTON, WILLIAM CALDWELL (1868-1952), PAPERS,
    1893-1951, 3 FT., RG 133

William Caldwell Johnston and Emily Logan Truax
Johnston were assigned to the PCUSA's West Africa
Mission in 1895. Their entire careers were spent in
West Africa where Reverend Johnston was instrumental
in developing a Presbyterian Church there. His service included work at Efulan, Elat and Yaounde. In
1921, he was named Field Secretary of the Presbyterian Mission in West Africa. He retired from mission service in 1938.

Arrangement: Series I. General Correspondence,
1895-1951; Series II. Personal Correspondence,
1897-1938; Series III. Official Correspondence,
1900-1901, and Station Minutes and Reports, 1902-
1938; Series IV. Miscellany, 1921-1938; Series V.
Diaries, 1894-1938.

16. LEITCH, ADDISON HARDIE (1908-), PAPERS, 1931-
    1933, 2 FOL.

Addison Hardie Leitch was appointed as a missionary
teacher to the Egypt Mission in 1931 by the UPCNA.
He resigned from missionary service in 1932.

Leitch's papers consist of outgoing correspondence,
1931-1932 which details his experiences as a teacher
in Assiut College and miscellaneous incoming correspondence, 1931-1933.

17. MCCAGUE FAMILY PAPERS, 1854-1886, .5 FT., RG 192

Thomas McCague (b.1825) and Henrietta Matilda Lowes
McCague (b.1832) were appointed as missionaries to
Egypt by the ARC in 1854. Until their return to the
United States in 1861, they taught and performed
evangelistic work in both Cairo and Alexandria.

Arrangement: Series I. Journal, Henretta McCague,

July-November, 1854; Series II. Correspondence
(typed transcripts), 1854-1868, 1886.

18. MYER/LAIRD FAMILY PAPERS, 1822-1834, 1 FOL.

Harriet Myer Laird (1803-1834) and Matthew Laird
(d.1834) were appointed by the Western Foreign Missionary Society in 1833 as missionaries to Liberia.
Their appointment marked the beginning of American
Presbyterian mission work in Africa. Four months
after their arrival, they died on the field of
dysentery.

This collection contains Harriet Myer Laird's family
correspondence and includes descriptions of her education, marriage and experiences in Liberia, 1822-
1834.

19. NASSUA, ROBERT HAMILL (1835-1921), PAPERS, 1880-
   1919, MF 3R

Robert Hamill Nassau was appointed in 1861 to the
PCUSA's Africa Mission. He was stationed at Corisco
Island until 1865, where he was superintendent of
the Girls' School. From 1865-1871, he was in charge
of the church at Benito, where he also engaged in
village itineration. In 1874, he commenced mission
work in the interior along the Ogowe River, estab-
blishing a station at Kangwe. His work took him
farther up river to Talaguga where he spent the period from 1882-1891. His later years were spent at
Libreville (1893-1898), where he served the Baraka
Church and Batanga (1900-1906). He retired from
missionary service in 1906.

This collection consists of two rolls of microfilm
containing Dr. Nassau's diaries, 1880-1919, and one
roll of undated "selected documents."

20. SCHWAB, GEORGE W. (1876-1955), PAPERS, 1905-
   1941, 2 FT., RG 57

21. SCHWAB, JULETTA HUELSTER (1879-1972), PAPERS,
   1914-1953, .5 FT., RG 164

George W. Schwab and Juletta Huelster Schwab were
appointed to the PCUSA's West Africa Mission in
1905, where they performed educational, industrial
and evangelistic work. Until 1920, they served in
Libreville, Elat, Metet and Batanga in French West
Africa. In 1920, they were assigned to explore the
entire Basa field. Until their retirement in 1941,

they served in Sakbayeme after the Basa field was
taken over by the PCUSA. They wrote extensively of
their experiences, including a monograph on the hin-
terland tribes of Liberia and several Bulu language
texts. Mr. Schwab was a research associate in an-
thropology for West Africa at Harvard University, a
Fellow of the Royal Geography Society, and a member of the American Academy of Political and Social
Sciences. Juletta H. Schwab, in addition to her
teaching and evangelistic duties, performed medical
work, wrote, edited, published and translated many
articles about Bulu life and culture.

Record group 57 consists of miscellaneous items that
reflect George Schwab's experiences in Africa, 1905-
1941.

Arrangement: Series I. Correspondence, Reports,
Diaries and Miscellaneous Items, 1905-1941.

Record Group 164 documents Juletta Schwab's experiences in Africa and reflects her observations about
African life and culture, notably the role of women
in Liberia.

Arrangement: Series I. Correspondence, Reports, and
Miscellaneous Items, 1914-1953.

22. THOMPSON, ANNA YOUNG (1851-1932), PAPERS, 1871-
    1931, 1 FT., RG 58

Anna Young Thompson was appointed as a missionary to
Egypt in 1872 under the UPCNA. Until her retirement
in 1931, she organized sabbath schools, taught young
girls and women and was instrumental in developing
the first Christian Endeavor Society in Egypt. She
was also responsible for organizing the World Christian Temperance Union, of which she served as national president for several years.

Arrangement: Series I. Correspondence and Diaries,
1872-1931; Series II. Miscellany, 1871-1931.

23. WATSON, ANDREW (1834-1916), DIARIES/NOTEBOOK,
    1860-1915, 33 V.

Andrew Watson was appointed to the UPCNA's Egypt
Mission in 1861 and served there until his death on
the field in 1916.

Watson's diaries cover the years 1860; 1872; 1874-
1879; 1882; 1890; 1899-1915; notebook circa 1880.

3. Adolphus C. Good, West Africa missionary, circa 1890.

4. George and Juletta Schwab, circa 1939.

5. Missionaries in the Cameroon, 1911. From left to right, George and Juletta Schwab, Danvers and Mary Love, Gayle Beanland.

6. Minniehaha Finney, [n.d.].

7. Anna Young Thompson, [n.d.].

LIAONING

SUIYUAN

CHAHAR   JEHOL

NINGHSIA

40   HOPEI

SHANSI

Peiping

Paoting

Tengchow   Chefoo

SHANTUNG

Shunteh   Tsinan

Wenhsien

Tsining   Ichow   Tungkao

Tengshsien

Y.hsuan

KANSU   35

CH'INGHAI

SHENSI   HONAN   KIANGSU

Nanhsuchow

Hwaiyuan

Showchow

Nanking

C H I N A   Scochow   Shanghai

SIKANG   SZECHUAN   HUPEH   ANHWEI   Hangchow   Yuyao

Nungpo   30

Kiukng   CHEKIANG

Taoyuan   Changteh

Changsha   KIANGSI

KWEICHOW   HUNAN

Siangtan

Hengchow   FUKIEN

Chenchow

YUNNAN   25

Linchow   KWANGTUNG

KWANGSI

Canton   Shekking

Yeungkong

BURMA   Kochow   20

FRENCH   Hoihow   Kiungchow
INDO-CHINA   Nodoa   Kachek

SIAM

MUIRHEAD, NEW YORK

CHINA MISSIONS

Stations and other points at which our MISSIONARIES
are located are shown by BLACK DOTS

THE BOARD OF FOREIGN MISSIONS
OF THE PRESBYTERIAN CHURCH IN THE U S A
156 FIFTH AVENUE NEW YORK

ASIA

China

Plans for Presbyterian mission work in China began
under the Western Foreign Missionary Society, though
no missionaries were actually appointed. Following
the organization of the PCUSA's Board of Foreign
Missions in 1837, the Reverend and Mrs. R.W. Orr and
the Reverend John A. Mitchell were appointed as the
first missionaries, arriving in Singapore in 1838.
Though this initial effort met with disaster, during
the course of the 19th and early 20th centuries the
China field was to become the PCUSA's largest missionary operation with eight distinct missions eventually being established. These included: the
South China Mission (1845); the Shantung Mission
(1862); the North China Mission (1863); the Hainan
Mission (1893); the Hunan Mission (1899); the Central China and Kiangnan Missions (1906) and the Yunnan Mission (1923). Missionaries from other Presbyterian denominations were also active in China
during this period. The UPCNA organized a mission
in Canton in 1860. PCUS missionaries commenced work
in Chekiang Province in 1867 while missionaries from
the CPC began work at Changteh in Hunan Province in
1897.

The PCUSA's station at Canton, begun in 1845, initially remained the only one in south China and because of its distance from the other stations was
organized as a separate mission. Subsequent stations were later opened at Yeungkong (1886); Linchow
(1890); Kochow (1912); and Sheklung (1915). Hainan,
originally an outgrowth of the Canton Mission, was
formally recognized as a separate mission in 1893
and included the stations at Nodoa, Kiungchow
(1884-1885), and Kachek (1902).

PCUSA missionary work in northern China centered
around Chefoo and began in 1862. The Shantung Mission, destined to become the largest mission in
China, included the stations at Tsinan (1872); Weih-
sien (1882); Ichow (1891); Tsining (1892); Tsingtao
(1898); Yihsien (1905); and Tenghsien (1913). Work
in Peiping commenced in 1863, with stations later
opened at Paoting (1893) and Shuntech (1903). These
three stations were later incorporated as the North
China Mission in 1905.

The opening of Siangtan in 1899 signaled the beginning of missionary work in the interior province of
Hunan. The advent of the Boxer Rebellion temporar-
ily disrupted work until 1902 when the station at
Hengchow was organized. Additional stations were
later opened at Chenchow (1904); Changteh (1906);
and Changsha (1913). The Yunnan Mission, formerly
part of the Siam Mission until 1923, consisted of
the stations at Chiengrun and Yuankiang. In 1933,
the former was returned to the Siam Mission, with
the remaining missionaries and churches being transferred to the German Vandsburger Mission.

The stations of the Central China Mission predated
the mission's formal establishment in 1906. Ningpo
became the first permanent station to be occupied in
1844, followed by stations at Shanghai (1850); Soo-
chow (1871); and Hangchow (1895), though Southern
Presbyterians had established a mission there in
1868. The stations of the Kiangnan Mission also
preceded the mission's formal organization and consisted of Nanking (1876); Hwaiyuan (1901); Nanhsuchow (1912); and Showchow (1919).

The PCUSA's ministry in China was educational, medical and evangelical in nature. Elementary, secondary, higher education and technical institutions
presented western ideas that challenged the tradi-
tional concept of a classic Chinese education.
Medical facilities like the McCartee Hospital, the
J.G. Kerr Hospital for the Insane and Ming Sam
School for the Blind exemplified the Church's concern for the physical well-being of the Chinese
people and eventually over ninety-two hospitals and
dispensaries were established throughout China.
Evangelization, though an integral part of the
PCUSA's educational and medical work, was a coopera-
tive effort between various Presbyterian groups
working in China. A synod was organized in 1906,
which in 1918 became the General Assembly of the
Presbyterian Church in China. In 1927, the latter

was renamed the Church of Christ in China and included representatives from different denominations
working in China.

Mission work in China was disrupted by the Kuomin-
tang in 1927 and by the Japanese invasion and occupation, 1937-1945. The advent of the 1949-1950
takeover by the Chinese Communists terminated missionary work on the Chinese mainland, though work
continued in conjunction with other denominations in
Hongkong and on Taiwan among the refugee populations.

                    * * * * *

24. BERCOVITZ, NATHANIEL (1889-1979), PAPERS, 1915-
    1951, 1 FOL.

Nathaniel Bercovitz and Elva Lorine Higgins Bercovitz were appointed to the PCUSA's Hainan Mission in
1915. As a medical missionary, Dr. Bercovitz served
as head of the American Presbyterian Hospital and
orphanage on the island of Hainan. He conducted a
number of medical studies which were published in
various Chinese medical journals. He was incarcerated by the Japanese in 1941 and again in 1950 by
the Chinese Communists. He returned to the United
States in 1953.

Dr. Bercovitz's papers consist of miscellaneous correspondence and notebooks, 1915-1951.

25. BOARD OF FOREIGN MISSIONS (PCUSA), RECORDS, SEC-
    RETARIES' FILES, CHINA MISSION, 1837-1957, [MF
    31 R., 1835-1911; 1891-1957, 74 FT., RG 82 & RG
    129]

The China Mission Secretaries' Files document the
work of the PCUSA's Board of Foreign in China,
1837-1957. The microfilmed materials consist of
outgoing/incoming correspondence, minutes and reports, 1837-1911. Record groups 82 and 129 consist
of similar materials that mainly date from 1911,
though earlier materials are also included.

26. BOONE, NELL BURGESS (1886-1973), PAPERS, 1937-
    1950, 1 FOL.

Nell Burgess Boone was appointed to the PCUSA's
China Mission with her husband, Wilmot D. Boone,
M.D., in 1911. They were assigned to the Shantung

Mission where she worked in conjunction with the
YWCA. In 1931, they were transferred to Shanghai
where they served in the Nantao Christian Institute.
Following the 1937-1938 Sino-Japanese War, they
started the Goodwill Industries as a means of postwar rehabilitation. She retired from missionary
service in 1949.

Nelle Boone's papers consist of miscellaneous correspondence, 1937-1950.

27. BRADSHAW, HOMER VERNON (1899-), PAPERS, 1937-1957, .5 FT, RG 188

Homer Vernon Bradshaw was appointed by the PCUSA as
a medical missionary to the South China Mission in
1928. His entire career was spent at Linhsien station were he headed the medical staff of the Van
Norden Memorial Hospital for Women. He also taught
surgery in the Hackett Medical College in Canton.
From 1942-1945, he served in the U.S. Air Force as a
flight surgeon with Chennault's Flying Tigers in
China. Following the war, he returned to missionary
service in China in his former capacity. In 1951,
he and his wife, Wilda Hockenberry Bradshaw, were
arrested and incarcerated by the Chinese Communists
until their release in 1955. Dr. Bradshaw retired
from mission work in 1964.

Arrangement: Series I. Correspondence [incoming and
outgoing], 1937-1951, bulk dates from 1948-1950;
Series II. Miscellany, 1942-1957.

28. CARPENTER, ALICE MARGARET (1897-1985), PAPERS, 1922-1980, .25 FT., RG 206

Alice Margaret Carpenter was appointed in 1922 to
the PCUSA's South China Mission. Until her evacuation from China in 1943, she served as a teacher at
the Ming Sum School for the Blind, the Pooi Ying
Middle School and the Turner Training School of
Nursing. She resigned from missionary service in
1945.

Arrangement: Series I. Correspondence, 1922-1943;
Series II. Photographs, 1900s-1980s; Series III.
Miscellany, 1930s-1980s.

29. DOBSON, WILLIAM HERVIE (1870-1965), PAPERS, 1893-1964, .50 FT., RG 204

William Hervie Dobson, M.D., was sent as a surgeon

to the Yeungkong Station in South China Mission in
1897. As the first Presbyterian missionary to learn
the Yeungkong dialect, Dobson worked in the Canton
region as an evangelist, surgeon and teacher until
his retirement from missionary service in 1940.

Arrangement: Series I. Correspondence, 1893-1904;
Series II. Daybooks, ca. 1897-1898; Series III.
Photographs, ca. 1897-1964; Series IV. Miscellany,
1897-ca. 1940.

30. GAYLEY, SAMUEL RANKIN (1828-1862), JOURNALS,
    1856, 3 FOL.

Samuel Rankin Gayley was appointed by the PCUSA as a
missionary to the Shanghai Mission in 1856. He served at Tengchow and died in service in 1862.

Samuel Rankin Gayley's journal (and transcript) describes his journey from New York to Shanghai in 1856
and includes observations on the trans-Atlantic
crossing, diverse aspects of Chinese culture and relations with missionaries from other denominations.
A second undated and incomplete journal describes
his journey to Hangchow.

31. GILMAN, FRANK PATRICK (1853-1918), PAPERS, 1885-
    1918, 2 FT., RG 56

Frank Patrick Gilman was appointed by the PCUSA to
the Hainan Mission in 1885. He died in service
there in 1918.

Frank Patrick Gilman's papers consist almost exclusively of his diaries with some correspondence about
his wife, Mary White Gilman.

Arrangement: Series I. Diaries/Correspondence,
1885-1918.

32. HAYES, JOHN DAVID (1893-1957), PAPERS, 1949-
    1957, 3 FOL.

John David Hayes and Barbara Kelman Hayes were appointed by the PCUSA to the China Mission in 1917.
Hayes was interned by the Chinese Communists in 1950
and released the following year. In 1957, he was
appointed as a missionary to Indonesia but was kill-
ed in an automobile accident shortly thereafter.

John David Hayes's correspondence consists mainly of

family letters, the bulk of which cover the period
1949-1951.

**33. KILLIE, CHARLES A.   (1856-1916), PAPERS, 1889-
    1907, 1 FOL.**

Charles A. Killie was appointed by the PCUSA in 1889
to the Shantung Mission. In 1899, he was transferred to Peiping in the North China Mission where he
taught and performed evangelistic work until his
death on the field in 1916.

Charles A. Killie's papers consist of newsletters,
reports and correspondence, 1889-1907.

**34. KUNKLE, JULIA POST MITCHELL (1878-1973), PAPERS,
    1913-1973, 1 FOL.**

Julia Post Mitchell was appointed to the PCUSA's
South China Mission in 1916 after having taught lit-
erature for three years at Canton Christian College.
In 1916, she married Presbyterian missionary John S.
Kunkle. Until her retirement in 1950, she taught at
several institutions, including Lingnan University,
Union Theological College and Sun Yat Sen Univer-
sity.

Her papers consist of miscellaneous correspondence
1913-1973.

35. LAUTENSLAGER FAMILY, PAPERS, 1922-1952, 2 FOL.

Roy S. Lautenslager (1889-1978) and Harriet Grace
Miller Lautenslager (1889-) were appointed by the
PCUSA to the East China Mission in 1922. They were
assigned to the Hangchow Christian College where
Rev. Lautenslager taught until 1928. Following the
College's nationalization in 1928, he was appointed
to head the new Political Science and History Department. When the Sino-Japanese War reached the
Hangchow area in December of 1937, the College was
closed but later reopened in Shanghai, where Lautenslager served as Professor of Political Science from
1939-1942. He was interned by the Japanese in
Shanghai in 1942 and repatriated the following year.
The Lautenslagers returned to Hangchow in 1947, but
with the increasing restrictions placed on Christian
work by the Communist government were forced to return to the U.S. in 1951. They retired from active
missionary service in 1954.

The Lautenslager papers consists mainly of family

correspondence, miscellaneous reports and clippings,
1922-1952.

36. MCCARTEE FAMILY, PAPERS, 1854-1900, .5 FT., RG
    177

Divie Bethune McCartee (1820-1900) was appointed by
the PCUSA as a medical missionary to China in 1843.
Arriving in Ningpo in 1844, he performed medical and
evangelistic work. In 1853, he married Juana M.
Knight (d. 1900), also a PCUSA missionary. McCartee
performed consular services in China until a regular
consulate was established there in 1857, and was
later appointed vice-consul to Japan in 1862. The
McCartees returned to Ningpo in 1865 to resume their
missionary work. They were transferred to the
Shanghai mission in 1872 but resigned shortly thereafter so that Dr. McCartee could join the Shanghai
consular staff as interpreter and assessor in the
Mixed Court. He served as professor in the Imperial
University of Tokyo and acted as secretary of the
Chinese legation in that city until 1877. In 1885,
McCartee was appointed counselor to the Japanese legation in Washington, D.C. Two years later, the
McCartees were appointed to the PCUSA's Japan Mission where they served until Dr. McCartee's retirement in 1900. A prolific writer, Dr. McCartee's
published works included treatises on Asian history,
linguistics, natural science, medicine, politics and
religion.

The McCartee Family Papers consist of outgoing correspondence about their missionary experiences and
Dr. McCartee's consular service, 1854-1906.

Arrangement: Series I. Correspondence of Divie
Bethune McCartee, 1854-1900; Series II. Correspondence of Juana Knight McCartee, 1854-1900.

37. MCILVAINE, JASPER SCUDDER (1844-1881), PAPERS,
    1858-1881, 3 FOL.

Jasper Scudder McIlvaine was appointed by the PCUSA
to the China Mission in 1868. Stationed initially
at Peiping, he itinerated at various places within
Shantung Province until his death on the field in
1881.

Jason McIlvaine Scudder's papers contains outgoing
family correspondence, 1858-1881.

38. MILLIGAN FAMILY PAPERS, 1900-1984, 4 FT., RG 199

Frank R. Milligan (1883-1961) and Aimee Boddy Milligan (1884-1974) were appointed by the Free Methodist
Church as missionaries to China in 1907 and served
as evangelists in Hunan Province until 1915. In
1908, they were appointed to the PCUSA's China Mission. Until 1929, Frank Milligan served as principal
of the Presbyterian Boys' High School and later
vice-principal of the Union Middle School while
Aimee Milligan engaged in evangelistic work with
Chinese women. In 1930, they were assigned to the
Christian Literature Society in Shanghai where Rev.
Milligan translated, edited and supervised the distribution of Christian literature while Aimee Milligan was instrumental in starting a Christian Broad-
casting Station. Because of increasing political
tensions, Frank Milligan returned to Shanghai alone
in 1941 and was subsequently interred by the Japanese until 1945. They returned to Shanghai but, as
a result of the Communist take-over, were transferred to the Philippine Mission in 1950.

Edith Milligan (1914-1985), daughter of Frank and
Aimee Milligan, earned a medical degree from the
Women's Medical College in Philadelphia and was appointed to the PCUSA's China Council in 1941. The
advent of the Second World War delayed her sailing
for China until 1943. From 1943-1945, she ministered to war victims and refugees in Hengyang, Kwei-
yang, Pichieh and Kweichow. She was in charge of
the Chenhsien Hospital in Hunan from 1946-1948.
Following a furlough in 1948 she attempted to return
to China but conditions there at that time militated
against it.

Arrangement: Series I. Milligan Family Correspondence, 1917-1984; Series II. Miscellany [Clippings,
Notebooks, Citations], 1902-1984; Series III. Photographs, 1900-1984.

39. MONINGER, MARY MARGARET (1891-1950), PAPERS, 1915-1918, 4 FOL.

Mary Margaret Moninger was appointed by the PCUSA to
the China Mission in 1915 and served there until
1942. She taught and performed evangelistic work at
Kachek, Kiungchow and Hoihow stations, in addition
to writing, editing and translating a number of Chinese language items.

Her papers consist of outgoing correspondence to her
family, 1915-1918.

40. POMMERENKE FAMILY PAPERS, 1907-1980, 2 FT., RG
    193

Herbert (1900-1978) and Jean Macpherson Pommerenke
(1895-) served as missionaries to China until their
retirement in 1970. Jean Macpherson was appointed
by the PCUSA as a teacher in 1920 to the True Light
Middle School in Canton. Herbert Pommerenke served
as a volunteer teacher at Linghan University in Canton from 1924-1927. They were married in 1927. In
1930, they were appointed to the China Mission where
they were assigned to the Yeungkong Station. They
were transferred to Kochow in 1934 where they taught
and performed evangelistic work. During 1937-1938,
Herbert Pommerenke taught at Union Theological Seminary in Canton before their reassignment to Yeungkong, where Jean Pommerenke taught in the primary
schools and Herbert Pommerenke performed evangelistic work. Their work was hampered in the late 1930s
by the Japanese invasion which resulted in their
capture, internment and repatriation in 1942. They
returned to Free China in 1943 where they were engaged in relief work in Chengtu. In 1946, they were
assigned to Canton to assist with the postwar rehabilitation and remained there until 1948 when they
were forced out by the Chinese Communists. They
were assigned to the Brazil Mission in 1952 where
Herbert Pommerenke served as Acting Treasurer of
that mission. They were assigned to Hongkong in
1955 where Herbert Pommerenke served as pastor of a
church comprised of Chinese refugees from the former
Presbyterian Mission on Hainan Island.

Arrangement: Series I. Correspondence, 1907-1980;
Series II. Miscellany, 1900-1960s.

41. RANKIN, HENRY VAN VLECK (1825-1863), PAPERS,
    1842-1863, 1 FT. RG 176

Henry Van Vleck Rankin was appointed to the PCUSA's
China Mission in 1848 and served at Ningpo. He died
on the field in 1863.

Arrangement: Series I. Correspondence, 1842-1863;
Series II. Diaries, 1846-1863; Series III. Miscellany, 1844-1863.

42. STROH, HARRIET (1896-), PAPERS, 1918-1970, 1.5
    FT., RG 187

Harriet Stroh was appointed to the PCUSA's China
Mission in 1919. She taught at the Girls' School

8. Dr. Divie Bethune McCartee, [n.d.].

9. Charles Killie in Chinese garb, 1893.

10. Henry Van Vleck Rankin, [n.d.].

11. Mary Margaret Moninger, [n.d.].

in Hwaiyuan (1920-1927; 1933-1937) and at the North
China American School (1927-1928). She performed
evangelistic work at Paoting (1928-1929), Hwaiyuan,
(1929-1931) and Showchow (1935-1936). She also engaged in refugee work at Hwaiyuan during the Sino-
Japanese War (1937- 1939). She resigned from mission service in 1942.

Arrangement: Series I. Correspondence, 1918-1957;
Series II. Photographs, 1924-1938; Series III. Miscellany, 1919-1970.

43. VAN DYCK FAMILY PAPERS, 1926-1959, 3 FOL.

David Bevier Van Dyck (1892-1963) and Anna Richard-
son Van Dyck (1895-) were appointed to the PCUSA's
China Mission in 1918 and were assigned to Hwaiyuan.
In 1927, Communist activities necessitated their
evacuation to Korea where they remained for several
months before relocating to Tsingtao on the Shantung
coast. In 1928, they returned to Hwaiyuan and from
1933-1940, worked in the Showchow field at Anhwei.
Mr. Van Dyck returned to Hunan in 1943, but was
forced to return to the U.S. in 1949-1950 following
the takeover by the Chinese Communists. The Van
Dycks retired from mission service in 1953.

The Van Dyck papers consist mainly of correspondence, reports and photographs, 1926-1959.

INDIA MISSIONS

Stations and other points at which
our MISSIONARIES are located
are shown by BLACK DOTS

MUIRHEAD NEW YORK

THE BOARD OF FOREIGN MISSIONS
OF THE PRESBYTERIAN CHURCH IN THE U S A
156 FIFTH AVENUE NEW YORK

India

The beginnings of American Presbyterian work in India date from 1834 when William Reed and John C.
Lowrie arrived in India under the auspices of the
Western Foreign Missionary Society and established a
station at Ludhiana. Two years later, stations were
opened by the PCUSA in Saharanpur, Sabathu and
Allahabad. In 1840, the India Mission was subdivided into the Punjab Mission, which encompassed the
original four stations, and the North India Mission,
also known as the Farukhabad Mission.

Other Presbyterian denominations were also active in
establishing missions in India. Missionaries from
the Associate Presbyterian Synod of North America
established a mission at Sialkot in 1854. This
mission was transferred to the UPCNA in 1858. Following the merger of the PCUSA and the UPCNA in
1958, the Sialkot Mission was transferred to the
newly formed UPCUSA. In 1904, the Calvinistic
Methodist Church in the U.S.A. appointed Dr. Thomas
John Jones to Silchar where he had served for ten
years under the Church in Wales. In 1920, the
CMCUSA's mission work in India was transferred to
the PCUSA following the merger of those two denominations.

The PCUSA's work in the Punjab throughout the nineteenth century revolved around the stations of Ludhiana, Saharanpur, Sabathu and Allahabad. Other
stations were opened at Khanna in 1908, followed by
Rupar in 1910, Moga in 1911 and Kasur in 1913. Work
at the North India Mission expanded considerably
throughout the late nineteenth and early twentieth
centuries. Mainpuri was opened in 1843, followed by

Fatehgarh in 1844, Jullundur in 1846 and Mussorie in
1847. Work at Dehra Dun and Fatehpur began in 1853,
followed by Etawah a decade later. Hoshyarpur was
occupied by PCUSA missionaries in 1867 and Etah in
1873, though the latter was not formally established
as a separate station until 1900. Work at Ferozepur
commenced in 1882, followed by Cawnpore in 1901,
Gwalior and Kasganj in 1911 and Shikohabad in 1924.
In 1870, the ABCFM's work in western India was
transferred to the PCUSA. Thereafter, that field
was known as the West India Mission. In addition to
the inherited station at Kolhapur, new stations were
begun at Ratnagiri in 1873, Sangli in 1874, Miraj in
1892, Kololi in 1893, Islampur in 1906 and Nipani in
1910.

The work of the PCUSA in India was educational,
medical and evangelical in nature. A variety of
educational institutions, either started by the
PCUSA or in which it cooperated with other denomina-
tions, were established. Some of these included
Ewing Christian High School; Allahabad College and
Agricultural Institute; Forman Christian College;
the North India School of Medicine for Christian
Women and the Isabella Thoburn College. Medical
work was carried out through a variety of hospitals,
dispensaries, clinics, sanitaria and leper asylums.
Institutions like the Wanless Chest Hospital in
Miraj, the Philadelphia Hospital in Ambala and the
Fatehgarh Memorial Hospital illustrate the medical
work performed by the PCUSA in India.

Evangelism in India took the form primarily of village itineration. Reflecting the PCUSA's policy of
encouraging the development of indigenous churches,
a Presbyterian Church in India was formed in 1904.
In 1924, this church along with the Congregationalist Church in West India merged to form the United
Church of Northern India. In 1970, the United
Church of Northern India joined with six other
churches and became known as the Church of Northern
India.

                    * * * * *

44. BOARD OF FOREIGN MISSIONS (PCUSA), RECORDS, SEC-
    RETARIES' FILES, INDIA MISSION, 1833-1972 [MF
    73 R, 1833-1910; 1891-1972, 35 FT., RG 83, 1 V.]

The India Mission Secretaries' Files consists of microfilmed outgoing/incoming correspondence, minutes
and reports, 1833-1910. Record group 83 consists

of similar materials dating from 1891-1972, though
most of the records date from 1911 through the late
1960s.

Arrangement: Series I. North India Mission, 1894-
1974; Series II. Punjab Mission, 1910-49; Series
III. West India Mission, 1911-49; Series IV. India
Mission, 1949-1972; Series V. Miscellany, 1891-
1966.

45. BOARD OF FOREIGN MISSIONS, (ARC/UPCNA), RECORDS, SIALKOT MISSION, 1856-1890, 4 V.

The records of the Sialkot Mission consist of annual
reports, 1856-1864 (3 v.) and minutes, 1856-1890 (1
v.).

46. BLACK, MARY HELEN (1894-), DIARIES, 1920-1970, 11 V.

Appointed to the PCUSA's Punjab Mission in 1918,
Mary Helen Black served as a teacher at the Dehra
Dun Girls' High School from 1921-1925 and as principal of that institution from 1926-1941. She returned to the U.S. at the outbreak of the Second
World War where she served under the Board of National Missions as a teacher at the Tucson Training
School. In 1945, she returned to India where she
served as principal of the Girls' Section of the
United Christian High School in Jullundur until
1947. The following year she continued her prewar
duties at Dehra Dun until her retirement in 1959.

Black's diaries cover the period from 1920-1970,
except for the years 1921 and 1923-1925. The eleven
volumes consist of short entries that reflect her
daily activities.

47. CAMPBELL FAMILY PAPERS, 1820-1864, 7 FOL., 1 V.

James Robinson Campbell (1800-1864) and Mary Cross
Campbell (d. 1880) were sent to India in 1835 by the
Reformed Presbyterian Church. In 1836, they transferred to the PCUSA. They were instrumental in establishing the mission station at Saharanpur in
1838. James Robinson Campbell and Mary Cross Campbell died on the field in 1864 and 1881 respectively.

Their family papers consist of outgoing correspondence 1820-1864 and James Robinson Campbell's journal, circa 1838.

**48. DENNIS, MAYE ANETTE (1887-1972), PAPERS, 1921-
    1940, 1 FOL.**

Maye Anette Dennis served as a teacher with the
Women's Board of Home Missions (1908-1914) before
entering foreign mission service. In 1917, she was
appointed to the PCUSA's North India Mission. She
taught at the Wanamaker High School in Allahabad
until 1919 when she was assigned to Mainpuri where
she performed zenana work and taught Hindu, Sikh,
Moslem and Christian women. She supervised the
Kharpari Conference Center for city evangelism and
inaugurated the Christian Opportunity Center in
Mainpuri, an evangelistic outreach service for
mothers, teachers, nurses, young people and rural
pastors. She retired from active mission work in
1952, but continued to serve in India for another
six years at the Holman Institute, a Methodist institution in Agra.

Maye Anette Dennis' papers consist of assorted reports and correspondence, 1921-1940.

**49. HAYES, MABELL SAMMONS (1895-1981), PAPERS, 1924-
    1981, 3 FT., RG 182**

Mabell Sammons Hayes was appointed as a medical missionary to the PCUSA's India Mission in 1924. She
served at Fatehgarh from 1925-1927. Until 1960, she
served as a physician on the staff of Allahabad
Agricultural Institute where her husband headed the
Horticulture Department. In 1960, she was sent to
the Punjab Synod, where she served on the staff of
the Ludhiana Christian Medical School until 1962.
She enrolled as a Peace Corps volunteer from 1965-
1967 and served with the Department of Social and
Preventative Medicine, SMS, Medical College, Jaipur,
Rajasthan. Until her return to the U.S. in 1970,
she served in Naila, a village in the Jaipur District, where she performed general clinic work and
lectured at the Health Center.

Dr. Hayes' papers consist of diaries, correspondence, photographs and albums that reflect her years
in India as a PCUSA medical missionary, a Peace
Corps volunteer and as a private citizen.

Arrangement: Series I. Diaries, 1924-1981; Series
II. Correspondence, 1926-1970; Series III. Photo-
graphs/photograph albums, 1925-1969; Series IV. Miscellany, 1924-1978.

49A.HILL, KATE ALEXANDER (1873-1960), PAPERS, 1896-1955, 2 FT., RG 53

Kate Alexander Hill was appointed as a missionary under the Woman's Board of the UPCNA in 1896. Until her retirement in 1943, she served as a teacher in the Lyallpur, Sangla Hill, Sargodha and Sialkot Districts in India.

Kate Alexander Hill's papers consist mainly of incoming and outgoing correspondence and scrapbooks, 1896-1942.

Arrangement: Series I. Correspondence/miscellaneous items, 1896-1955; Series II. Scrapbooks, 1896-1955.

50. JANVIER FAMILY PAPERS, 1804-1964, 2.5 FT., RG 190

The Janvier Family served the PCUSA for three generations as missionaries to India. This service commenced in 1841 with the appointment of Levi Janvier and concluded in 1957 with the retirement of Ernest and Alma Janvier.

Levi Janvier (1816-1864), son of George Washington Janvier (1784-1865), and his first wife, Hannah Janvier (d. 1854), were appointed to the PCUSA's India Mission in 1841. Following his wife's death, Levi Janvier married Mary Rankin Porter, the widow of missionary Joseph Porter. In 1864, Rev. Janvier was murdered by a Sikh fanatic at Sabathu. Mary Rankin Janvier retired from mission service in 1875.

Caesar Augustus Rodney Janvier (1861-1928), son of Levi and Mary Rankin Janvier, was appointed in 1887 to the India Mission with his wife, Susan Rankin Janvier (1858-1943). They served in Fatehgarh until 1901 when Rev. Janvier was called to the Holland Memorial Presbyterian Church in Philadelphia. They returned to India in 1913 where Rev. Janvier served as principal of Ewing Christian College until his death in 1928. Susan Rankin Janvier retired from mission work in 1930.

Ernest Paxton Janvier (1890-1962) and Alma Thornton Johnson Janvier (1891-) were appointed to the PCUSA's North India Mission in 1920. The son of Caesar Augustus Rodney and Susan Rankin Janvier, he was assigned initially to educational work in Fatehgarh and later taught at Ewing Christian College and the Mary Wanamaker School in Allahabad.

12. Mary Helen Black, [n.d.].

13. Maye Anette Dennis, [n.d.].

14. Sir William James Wanless, [n.d.].

15. Mabel Sammons Hayes, 1918.

16. Kate Alexander Hill, [n.d.].

Though his primary interests were literature distribution and evangelistic work, he also wrote, edited,
and translated a number of Hindu language items.
They retired from missionary service in 1957.

The Janvier Family Papers consist of correspondence,
reports, photographs, and miscellaneous items, 1804-
1964, though the bulk of the collection dates from
1850-1957.

Arrangement: Series I. George Washington Janvier,
1804; 1864; Series II. Levi Janvier, 1850-1862;
Series III. Mary Rankin Janvier, 1825-1862; Series
IV. Caesar Augustus Rodney Janvier, 1898-1929; Se-
ries V. Susan Rankin Janvier, 1915-1937; Series VI.
Ernest Paxton Janvier, 1921-1957; Series VII. Alma
Thornton Janvier, 1962; Series VIII. Photographs,
circa 1900-1950; Series IX. Miscellany, 1841-1964.

51. MARSHALL, MARY STEWART (1872-1961), PAPERS,
    1900-1934, 1 FOL.

Mary Jane Stewart, M.D., was appointed to the
PCUSA's West India Mission in 1899. In 1902, she
married Rev. Alexander W. Marshall of the same mission. Until her retirement in 1934, she performed
medical and evangelistic work in Kolhapur.

Dr. Marshall's papers consist of miscellaneous correspondence, 1900-1934.

52. MITCHELL, ALICE (1862-1916), PAPERS, 1893-1905,
    2 FOL.

Alice Mitchell, M.D., the daughter of Board of Foreign Missions Secretary Arthur Mitchell, was appointed to the PCUSA's India Mission as a medical
missionary in 1895. Her entire term of service was
spent in Mussoorie at the Woodstock School and College of which she became principal in 1914. She
died in service in 1916.

Dr. Mitchell's papers consist of primarily outgoing
correspondence, 1893-1895 and 1904-1905.

53. PARKER FAMILY PAPERS, 1923-1947, 4 V.

Edwin Graham Parker (1894-1963) and Ruth Rubin Parker (1894-) were appointed to the PCUSA's India Mission in 1923. Until their retirement in 1960, they
taught and performed evangelistic work in Fatehgarh
and Etah.

The Parker Family Papers consists of four volumes of
primarily outgoing correspondence to family members
and friends and incoming correspondence of Ruth
Parker from Edwin G. Parker, 1923-1947.

Arrangement: Series I. Correspondence, 1923-1947
[v. 1, 1923-1929; v. 2, 1929-1937; v. 3, 1938-1942;
v. 4, 1942-1947]

54. PRENTICE FAMILY PAPERS, 1926-1954, .5 FT., RG
    191

John Wilbur Prentice (1901-1962) and Mary Agnes Lefker Prentice (1896-) were appointed to the PCUSA's
India Mission in 1926. Initially stationed at
Saharanpur where Rev. Prentice taught at the Theological Seminary, they spent the next two years engaged in rural evangelism in Etawah and Etah. In
1929, they were assigned to Allahabad Christian College where Rev. Prentice taught and served as treasurer of that institution and Mary Agnes Lefker Prentice taught in the Jumna Primary School and the Mary
Wanamaker School. In 1940, Rev. Prentice was appointed treasurer of the India Mission Council and
served in the Inter-Mission Business Office in Bom-
bay until 1952. In that year, they returned to
Allahabad Christian College where they served until
their retirement in 1961.

The Prentice Family Papers consist of outgoing correspondence, personal labor reports and miscellaneous items, 1926-1954.

Arrangement: Series I. Reports, 1928-1953; Series
II. Correspondence, 1926-1937; 1953-1954; Series
III. Miscellany, 1933; 1946.

55. WANLESS, WILLIAM JAMES (1865-1933), PAPERS,
    1889-1933, 1.5 FT., RG 92

Dr. William James Wanless was appointed as a medical
missionary to the PCUSA's India Mission in 1889. He
began his work at Sangli but in 1892 moved to Miraj
where he was to remain until his retirement in 1931.
His skill and ability as an evangelist, physician
and surgeon drew patronage and support that resulted
in the establishment of hospitals, leper asylums and
a tuberculosis sanitarium. For his service to the
people of India, Dr. Wanless was thrice decorated by
the Indian government and in 1928 was knighted by
the British government.

Arrangement: Series I. Personal Correspondence,
1924-1929; Series II. Correspondence with BFM,
1892-1931; Series III. General Correspondence,
1892-1933; Series IV. Miscellany, 1905-1931; Series V. Diaries/Scrapbooks/Miscellaneous Notebooks,
1889-1925.

JAPAN AND CHOSEN MISSIONS

Stations and other points at which our MISSIONARIES are located are shown by BLACK DOTS

THE BOARD OF FOREIGN MISSIONS OF THE PRESBYTERIAN CHURCH IN THE U S A 156 FIFTH AVENUE. NEW YORK

Japan

Presbyterian mission work in Japan commenced shortly
after the conclusion of the 1854 Japanese-American
treaty negotiated by Commodore Matthew Perry. In
1855, the PCUSA sent Dr. Divie B. McCartee of the
China Mission to Japan to determine the feasibility
of beginning mission work there. McCartee's efforts
to reach Japan were thrice aborted. In 1858, the
Board of Foreign Missions appointed Dr. James and
Clara M. Lette Hepburn as the first Presbyterian
missionaries to Japan. Their arrival in Yokohama in
October of the following year marked the beginnings
of the PCUSA's work there.

Mission work by the PCUS began in 1855 at Kochi on
the island of Shikolu and later at Nagoya. The
areas around these centers, together with Kobe where
a theological seminary was started in 1907, were the
main areas of the PCUS's missionary work. Missionaries from the Reformed Church in America commenced
mission work in Nagasaki in 1859. In 1876, the Cumberland Presbyterian Church began its mission in
Japan at Osaka and grew steadily under the leadership of the Hail families. Following the 1906 merger between the Cumberland Church and the PCUSA, the
work at Osaka, Wakayama and Tsu stations was transferred to the PCUSA.

Early missionary endeavors in Japan were beset by
considerable difficulties. The missionaries were
regarded with suspicion and dislike. Their motives
were misunderstood and purpose misrepresented. Con-
versions were especially difficult given the overwhelmingly Buddhist population. Social ostracism
and persecution awaited those who became Christians.

This xenophobia subsided after 1896 and by the start
of the twentieth century its forces had been spent.

Despite the hostility experienced by all Presbyterian missionaries throughout the closing decades of
the nineteenth century, expansion of the PCUSA's
activities did continue, albeit at a slow pace. In
1869, Tokyo station was opened, followed by Osaka in
1877. Work in Kanazawa, the largest city on the
west coast and a stronghold of conservative Bud-
dhism, was started in 1879. Although work had been
started in Hiroshima in 1883, a station was not formally established there until 1887. Hokkaido station was organized the same year, followed by Kyoto
in 1890. Yamaguchi, which merged in 1935 with Hiroshima to become the Sanyo station, was occupied in
1891 as was Fukui, though the latter was closed by
the Board of Foreign Missions in 1923. Work at Ota-
ru commenced in 1894, followed by Matsuyama and Asa-
higawa in 1900 and Nokkeushi in 1914.

The PCUSA's work in Japan was primarily educational
and evangelistic in nature. The existence of an extensive system of government and privately supported
primary schools and hospitals made the PCUSA's work
in these areas unnecessary. The lack of adequate
secondary and higher education facilities for girls
and young women resulted in the PCUSA's establishment of several institutions, including Joshi Gakuin
(1873), Wilmina Jo Gakuin (1907) and the Woman's
Christian College (1918). The PCUSA also conducted
ten kindergartens, a boys' middle school, a college
(Meiji Gakuin) and an Oral School for the Deaf. The
PCUSA also cooperated with other denominations in
the operations of two theological seminaries.

The beginnings of an indigenous Presbyterian church
in Japan date from 1872 when the first local church
was organized in Yokohama. In 1877, representatives
of the PCUSA, the Reformed Church in America and the
United Presbyterian Church of Scotland established
the United Church of Christ in Japan, of which the
PCUS and Reformed Church in the United States eventually became members.

                    * * * * *

56. BOARD OF FOREIGN MISSIONS (PCUSA/UPCUSA), RE-
    CORDS, SECRETARIES' FILES, JAPAN MISSION, 1859-
    1972, [MF 23 R., 1859-1911; 1879-1972, 18 FT.,
    RG 93]

The Secretaries' Files for the Japan Mission documents the work of the PCUSA/UPCUSA in Japan, 1859-
1972. The microfilmed materials include outgoing
and incoming correspondence, minutes and reports for
the East and West Japan Missions, 1859-1911. Record
group 93 consists of a variety of reports, correspondence, minutes, 1879-1972, though the bulk of
its contents dates from 1911 through the late 1960s.

Arrangement: Series I. Minutes, 1911-1955; Series
II. Reports, 1911-1972; Series III. Correspondence,
1879-1971; Series IV. Interboard Committee for
Christian Work in Japan, 1950-1970; Series V. Miscellany, 1892-1972.

17. Japanese Sunday School class, 1902.

Korea (Chosen)

Presbyterian mission work in Korea (Chosen) began in
1884 when Dr. Horace and Frances Messenger Allen of
the PCUSA's Shanghai station were transferred to
Pyengyang. Eventually seven additional stations
were established, including Taiku (1889); Syenchyun
(1901); Chairyung (1906); Chungju (1908); Andong
(1910); and Hingking in Manchuria (1918). Mission
work in Korea was done in cooperation with several
other denominations including the PCUS, which had
entered Korea in 1892 and occupied the southwest
corner of the peninsula; Canadian and Australian
Presbyterians; as well as Methodists, Baptists,
Anglicans and Methodist Episcopalians. Presbyterians and Methodists were the two largest denominations operative in Korea. In 1907, the Presbyterian groups established the Union Presbyterian
Church in Korea with the first General Assembly
being held in 1912.

Medical work played a prominent role in the PCUSA's
missionary efforts in Korea. In 1885, Dr. Allen
founded the Royal Korean Hospital in Seoul which
eventually became the Severance Union Hospital/Medi-
cal College and Nurses Training School. In 1896, a
hospital was established in Pyengyang in cooperation
with the Methodists. The church's educational work
in Korea commenced rather late and was beset by a
variety of difficulties, one of which was language.
Primary schools, academies for boys and girls, a
theological seminary and several colleges were eventually developed. The theological seminary in Seoul
was an interdenominational effort with the

Methodists as were the Pierson Memorial Bible
School, the Christian Literature Society and the
Union Language School.

Mission work in Korea was complicated by several
factors uncommon to other missions. The presence of
the Japanese after 1910 and until 1945 did much to
undermine the work of the church, particularly during the 1930s. The Shrine Issue, though superfi-
cially a political concern, sought to reduce the
role of the church in Korea to the will of the Japa-
ese Emperor. The divisiveness that it caused was
clearly manifested both before and after the Second
World War. Likewise, the Korean War, together with
schisms within the Korean Presbyterian Church, pro-
duced a period of retrenchment from which the effects are still being felt.

                    * * * * *

57. ADAMS, EDWARD (1895-1965), PAPERS, 1937-1941, 1
    FOL.

Edward Adams and Susan Comstock Adams were appointed
to the PCUSA's Korea Mission in 1920. In 1925,
Edward Adams was appointed principal of the Taiku
Bible Institute. Following his work with refugees
during the 1950s, he was appointed president of
Keimyung Christian College, a position that he held
until his retirement in 1963.

Edward Adams' papers consist of miscellaneous correspondence and reports, 1936-1941.

58. BAIRD, ANNIE LAURIE (1864-1916), PAPERS, 1890-
    1916, .5 FT., RG 172

59. BAIRD, WILLIAM M. (1862-1931), PAPERS, 1885-
    1931, 1 FT., RG 173

William M. Baird, M.D., and Annie Laurie Baird were
appointed to the PCUSA's Korea Mission in 1890.
Until 1897, they served at Seoul, Fusan and Taiku
stations. They were transferred to Pyengyang in
1897 where Dr. Baird was appointed president of the
Pyengyang Academy and Union Christian College, a
position that he held until his death in 1931.
Annie Laurie Baird conducted the first woman's Bible
Training class in Pyengyang and assisted Dr. Baird
with his work at the college. She also prepared a
Korean language text for new missionaries, published
several works on Korean life and translated a number

of other articles.   She died in service in Pyengyang in 1916.

Annie Laurie Baird's papers consist of personal correspondence, 1890-1916, though most of her letters
dated from 1890-1905.

Arrangement: Series I. Correspondence and miscellaneous items, 1890-1916.

William Baird's papers consists of diaries, correspondence, reports, and miscellaneous items, 1885-
1931.

Arrangement: Series I. Diaries, 1892-1895; Series
II. Correspondence, 1885-1916; Series III. Reports,
1891-1931; Series IV. Clippings/miscellaneous items,
1891-1931.

60. **BOARD OF FOREIGN MISSIONS (PCUSA/UPCUSA), RE-
    CORDS, SECRETARIES' FILES, KOREA MISSION, 1884-
    1972 [MF 16 R., 1884-1911; 1903-1972, 19 FT., RG
    140]**

The Secretaries' Files of the Korea Mission reflect
the PCUSA/UPCUSA's evangelical, educational and
medical work in Korea, 1884-1972.   The microfilmed
materials consist of outgoing and incoming correspondence, minutes and reports, 1884-1911.   Record
Group 140 consists of similar materials covering the
period from 1903-1972, though the bulk dates from
1911.

Arrangement: Series I. Reports, 1911-1971; Series
II. Correspondence, 1909-1972; Series III. Educa-
tional Work, 1903-1972; Series IV. Bible Institute/
Evangelism/Sunday schools/Youth and Rural Work,
1911-1971; Series V. Medical Work/Institutions,
1911-1971; Series VI. Korea Conspiracy/ Korean
Independence Movement, 1911-1971; Series VII. Mis-
sion School Certification Controversy/Academic
Maintenance Fund/Shrine Question, 1912-1943; Series
VIII. Mission College Controversy, 1905-1925;
Series IX. Presbyterian Church in Korea/Church and
Mission Ministry to Chinese and Japanese, 1903-1972;
Series X. Mission Property, 1911-1972;   Series XI.
Miscellany, 1907-1971.

61. **CLARK, CHARLES ALLEN (1878-1961), PAPERS, 1917-
    1925, 1 FOL.**

Charles Allen Clark and Mabel N. Craft Clark

(1876-1946) were appointed to the PCUSA's Korea
Mission in 1902. They were stationed in Seoul until
1923 and thereafter in Pyengyang until Mabel Clark's
death in 1946. Charles Allen Clark served as President of the Korea Theological Seminary where he also
taught until his retirement in 1948.

Clark's papers consist of outgoing correspondence
1917-1925.

62. KERR, WILLIAM CAMPBELL (1883-1976), PAPERS, 1946, 1 FOL.

William Campbell Kerr was appointed to the PCUSA's
Korea Mission in 1908. Until 1919, he was engaged
in evangelistic work with the country's increasing
Japanese-speaking population. In 1919, he was
transferred to the Japanese Mission and until his
internment in 1942, engaged in evangelistic work in
Kure and Seoul. In 1943, he assisted the U.S. Army
in a civilian capacity under the auspices of the
PCUSA and helped to facilitate the return of Prot-
estant missionaries to postwar Japan. During the
Korean War, he worked in the rehabilitation of North
Korean POWs via the POW Education Program of the
United Nations. He retired from missionary service
in 1955.

Kerr's papers consist of outgoing correspondence to
family members, 1946.

63. SMITH FAMILY PAPERS, 1911-1949, .25 FT., RG. 208

Roy Kenneth Smith, M.D., (1885-1958) and Lura Wilma
McLane Smith (1885-1979) were appointed to the
PCUSA's Korea Mission in 1911 and until their repatriation to the United States in 1942, performed
medical and evangelistic work in Andong, Taiku,
Chairyung, Seoul, Pyengyang and Syenchun. Dr. Smith
returned alone to Korea in 1946 as an employee of
the War Department to serve as Director of Tuberculosis Sanitoriums, a position that he held until
1948 when his government service ended. The Smiths
resumed their medical work at Taegu that same year
until their retirement from missionary service in
1950.

The Smith Family Papers consists of correspondence,
personal reports, photographs and miscellaneous
items which document their missionary service in
Korea, 1911-1949.

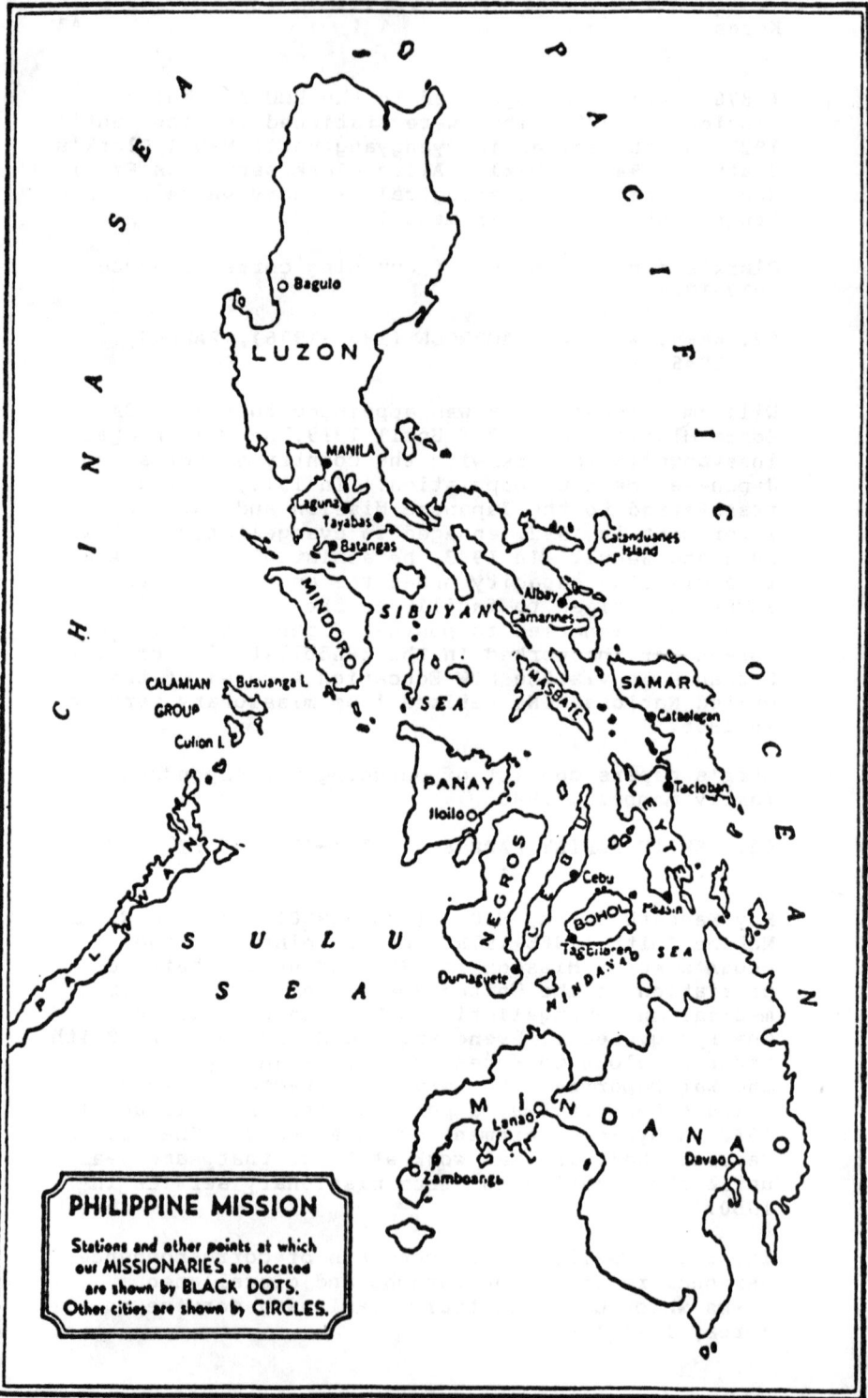

PHILIPPINE MISSION

Stations and other points at which
our MISSIONARIES are located
are shown by BLACK DOTS.
Other cities are shown by CIRCLES.

Philippines

Presbyterian mission work in the Philippines began
shortly after Admiral Dewey's victory in Manila in
1898. By April of 1899, missionaries had begun arriving in the Philippines and by January of 1900, a
Filipino Church had been organized and the Mission
was formally established. The PCUSA was first Protestant denomination to recognize the duty of American Christians to provide spiritual guidance to the
Filipino peoples. In 1901, the Executive Committee
of the Board of Foreign Missions called a conference
in Manila with representatives from the ABCFM, the
Baptist Missionary Union, the Missionary Society of
the Methodist Episcopal Church, the Board of Foreign
and Domestic Mission of the Protestant Episcopal
Church and the Board of Foreign Missions of the Reformed Church in America to formulate a strategy of
evangelization for the Philippines. This conference
resulted in the creation of the Evangelical Union of
the Philippine Islands, the purpose of which was to
unite all evangelical forces operative in the Philippines. Originally comprised of Methodists, Presbyterians, United Brethren, Baptists and Congregationalists, the Union was reconstituted in 1929 as
the National Christian Council and included representatives of the Baptists, Disciples of Christ,
Methodists and the United Evangelical Missions
(Presbyterians, Congregationalists and United Brethren) as well as the American Bible Society and the
Women's Christian Temperance Union.

As a result of the 1901 accord, Presbyterian work in
the Philippines encompassed several stations on the
islands of Luzon, Negros, Leyte, Panay and Samar. On
Luzon, stations were established in Laguna (1902),

Albay (1903), Tayabas (1905), the Camarines (1911),
Batangas (1917) and in Manila, which had first been
occupied in 1899 and was later divided equally between the Presbyterian and Baptist missions. On the
island of Negros, a station was opened in Dumaguete
(1901) while stations on Cebu and Bohol were started
in 1902 and 1909 respectively. Tacloband on the island of Leyte was opened in 1903 while Iloilo on
Panay was jointly occupied by both the Presbyterian
and Baptist missions until 1925. On Samar, the station at Catbalogan was occupied in 1930. The
PCUSA's ministry in the Philippines was medical, educational and evangelical in nature. Medical work
was first initiated in Iloilo in 1900 with hospitals, dispensaries and nurses' training facilities
established at Albay, Bohol, Dumaguete and Tacloban.
Because of the elaborate and costly educational program established by the American occupation, the
PCUSA limited its educational efforts to three institutions. These included Silliman University in
Dumaguete, the first Protestant school established
in the Philippines; the Ellinwood Bible School and
Union Theological Seminary, established in 1899 and
1907 respectively and located in Manila.

The PCUSA encouraged the Filipino Church to be self-
supporting and its plans for evangelizing the vast
interior regions were contingent upon this concept.
Evangelization was conducted via weekend and bi-
monthly Bible institutes, annual vacation bible
schools, kindergarten instruction and informal home
visitations. In 1948, the Presbyterian, Congregationalist, United Brethren and Philippine Methodist
churches formed the Philippine United Church.
Though the goal of the PCUSA had been to establish a
self-supporting indigenous church in the Philippines
this has not yet been realized. Although the Filipino people are for the most part at the head of
their churches, these churches and their related institutions are still heavily dependent on support
from the U.S. and other countries.

* * * * *

64. BOARD OF FOREIGN MISSIONS (PCUSA), RECORDS, SEC-
    RECRETARIES' FILES, PHILIPPINE MISSION, 1898-
    1973 [MF 3 R., 1898-1910; 1903-1972, 19 FT., RG
    85]

The Secretaries' Files of the Philippine Mission
document the medical, educational and evangelistic
work of the PCUSA, 1898-1973. The microfilmed ma-

terial consists of outgoing and incoming correspondence, 1898-1910. Record group 85 is comprised of
minutes, reports and correspondence, 1903-1973,
though the bulk of its contents date from 1910.

Arrangement: Series I. Minutes, 1911-1964; Series
II. Reports, 1911-1972; Series III. Correspondence,
1904-1971; Series IV. Miscellany, 1903-1973.

65. DOLTZ, PAUL (1875-1943), PAPERS, 1902-1941, 1 FT., RG 171

Paul Doltz and Clara McDermid Doltz were appointed
to the PCUSA's Philippine Mission in 1902. They
were assigned to Iloilo station where they engaged
in evangelistic work until 1916. In that year, they
were transferred to Dumaguete where Paul Doltz was
appointed Vice President and student pastor of Silliman University. They retired from mission work in
1936.

Paul Doltz's papers consist of correspondence,
printed materials, sermons, notes, clippings and
assorted photographs, 1902-1941.

Arrangement: Series I. Photographs, 1902-1930?
Series II. Correspondence and miscellaneous items,
1902-1941.

18. Paul and Clara Doltz commencing a tour, San Jose, Philippine Islands, 1912.

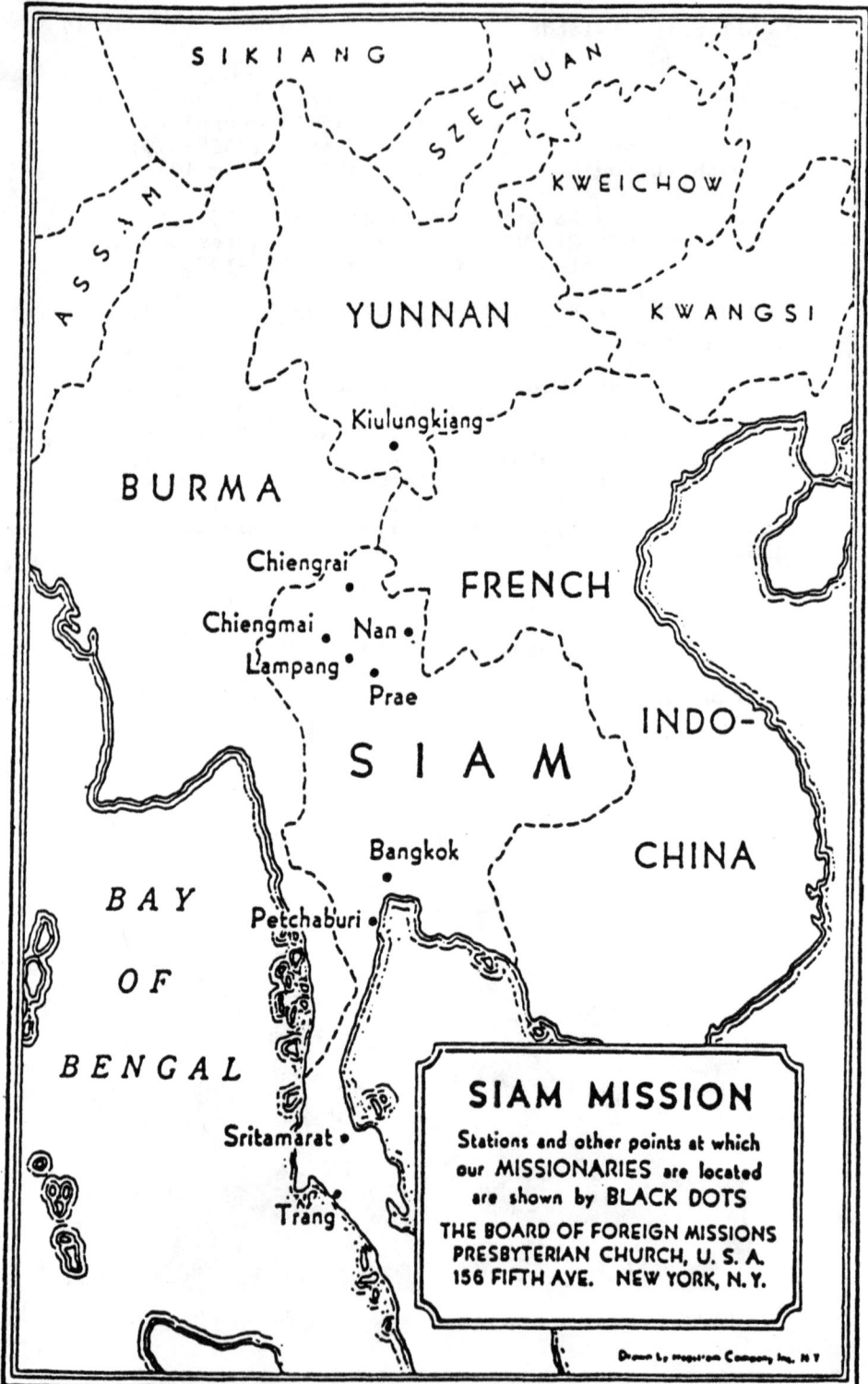

SIKIANG

SZECHUAN

KWEICHOW

ASSAM

YUNNAN

KWANGSI

BURMA

Kiulungkiang

Chiengrai

FRENCH

Chiengmai   Nan

Lampang

Prae

INDO-

SIAM

CHINA

Bangkok

BAY

Petchaburi

OF

BENGAL

Sritamarat

Trang

SIAM MISSION

Stations and other points at which
our MISSIONARIES are located
are shown by BLACK DOTS

THE BOARD OF FOREIGN MISSIONS
PRESBYTERIAN CHURCH, U. S. A.
156 FIFTH AVE.   NEW YORK, N. Y.

Drawn by magatron Company, Inc., N Y

Thailand (Siam)

Presbyterian interests in Thailand began in 1838
when the Reverend R.W. Orr of the China Mission
visited Bangkok and strongly urged the opening of a
mission there. In 1840, the PCUSA appointed Rev.
and Mrs. W.P. Buell to Siam to formally commence
mission work. The PCUSA was the only Presbyterian
denomination to conduct mission work in Siam.

Prior to 1878, work in Siam commenced slowly. Gov-
ernmental opposition to the missionaries characteri-
zed the first several years of the mission's existence, though by the mid 1850s much of this initial
resistence had subsided. During this period, only
two stations had been established: Petchaburi in
1860 and Chiengmai in 1867. Following the issuance
of the "Proclamation of Religious Liberty" in 1878
by the monarch, a period of rapid religious expansion followed. Between 1885 and 1917 eleven additional stations were opened.

Prior to 1922, two Presbyterian missions existed in
Siam. The North Siam Mission, often referred to as
the North Laos Mission, centered around Chiengmai
and became the springboard for stations that were
later established in Lampang, Lampun, Chiengrai,
Prae, Nan, Kengtung and Chiengrun. The South Siam
Mission, which was closely associated with Bangkok,
encompassed the stations of Pitsanuloke, Petchaburi,
Rajaburi, Sritamarat and Trang. The isolation of
the North and South Siam Missions ended in 1922 when
the railroad line reached Chiengrai, thus enabling
the two missions to merge. Thereafter, they were

referred to as the Siam (later Thailand) Mission.

The nature of the PCUSA's work in Siam was educational, medical and evangelical. The period of rapid religious expansion that began in the closing
decades of the nineteenth century continued into the
twentieth century. Educational facilities such as
Bangkok Christian College, the Harriet House School,
Wattana Wittaya Academy, Dara Academy and McGilvary
Theological Seminary were established as part of the
church's educational ministry. Dispensaries and
hospitals such as McCormick Hospital and the leper
asylums in Chiengmai and Sritamarat accompanied the
opening of every mission station.

In 1932, the presbyteries of North and South Siam
were released from the Synod of New York so that
they might form a national church. Two years later,
the first General Assembly of the new church met in
Bangkok and adopted a constitution. The name "The
Church of Christ in Siam" was adopted with the hope
that all Protestant bodies operative in Siam would
become members of this autonomous national church.
Since the end of World War II, this national church
has worked closely with the PCUSA/UPCUSA to continue
the church's work in Thailand.

                    * * * * *

66. BOARD OF FOREIGN MISSIONS (PCUSA/UPCUSA), RE-
    CORDS, SECRETARIES' FILES, THAILAND MISSION,
    1840-1973, [MF 14 R., 1840-1910; 1849-1973,
    18 FT., 13 V., RG 84]

The evangelistic, educational and medical work of
the PCUSA and the UPCUSA in Thailand is reflected in
this collection. The microfilmed material consists
of outgoing/incoming correspondence, minutes and
reports of the North and South Siam Mission, 1840-
1910. Record group 84 is comprised of similar materials and covers the period from 1865-1973, though
the bulk of its contents date from 1911.

Arrangement: Series I. North Siam Mission, 1865-
1920; Series II. South Siam Mission, 1911-1922; Series III. Siam/Thailand Mission, 1921-1973; Series
IV. North Laos Mission Minutes, 1872-1899; Treasurer's Records, 1900-1902; North Laos Presbytery
Minutes, 1885-1920; Series V. Bangkok Station
Minutes, 1849-1880; 1925-1931; Petchaburi Station
Minutes, 1887-1910; Pitsanuloke Station Minutes,
1917-1927; Series VI. Siam Presbytery Minutes,

1858-1888; 1909-1917; Series VII. Letters to Siam
Mission, 1847-1884.

67. CALLENDAR, CHARLES R. (1867-1952), PAPERS,
    1907-1913, 2 V.

Charles R. Callendar and N. Winella Marks Callendar
were appointed to the PCUSA's Siam Mission in 1896.
During their first term, they were assigned to La-
kawn Station where they engaged in evangelistic
work. In 1905, they were assigned to Kengtung,
Burma to work with the Thai in that area. Ill
health forced their resignation in 1907 but in 1909
they returned to Siam for service in Lampang. In
1920, they were transferred to the Kiulingkian station, Yunnan Province, China where they served until
their retirement in 1937.

This collection consists of two letterpress books,
1907-1913 which contains Charles R. Callendar's outgoing correspondence and other miscellaneous items.

68. CORT, EDWIN CHARLES (1879-1950), PAPERS, 1945-
    1946, 2 FOL.

69. CORT, MABEL GILSON (1872-1955), PAPERS, 1904-
    1944, 1 FOL.

Edwin Charles Cort was appointed as a medical missionary to the PCUSA's Siam Mission in 1908. Following two years of service at Lampang and Prae, he
was transferred to Chiengmai where he remained for
the duration of his career. In 1910, he married
fellow missionary Mabel Gilson. Dr. Cort was associated with McCormick Hospital which he helped to
develop into a fully equipped modern facility. He
also supervised the Leper Home in Chiengmai.

Dr. Cort's papers consist of correspondence dealing
primarily with the publication of his manuscript,
Yankee Thai, an autobiography about his experiences
in Siam.

Mabel Gilson was appointed to the PCUSA's Siam Mission in 1903. Throughout her career, she worked
mainly as a teacher, beginning in 1905 at Prince
Royal College and the Chiengmai Girls School. In
1923, she helped to start the Nurses Training School
at McCormick Hospital where she also taught and served as dietician for that institution. She and her
husband, Dr. Charles Cort, retired from missionary
service in 1949.

Mabel Gilson Cort's papers consists of outgoing
correspondence to family and friends, 1904-1944.

70. HOUSE, SAMUEL REYNOLDS (1817-1899), PAPERS, 1845-1872, 1 V., 3 FOL.

Samuel Reynolds House was appointed to the PCUSA's
Siam Mission in 1845 and was the first medical missionary designated to serve there. Following his
marriage to Harriet M. Pettit in 1855, Dr. House
returned to Siam where he performed medical work
until his retirement in 1876.

Samuel Reynolds House's papers consist of journals
and diaries that reflect his experiences as a medical missionary in Siam, 1845-1859 and correspondence
to his family and friends, 1846-72.

71. MCFARLAND, SAMUEL GAMBLE (1830-1897), PAPERS, 1876-1882, 1 V.

Samuel Gamble McFarland and Jane Hays McFarland were
appointed to the PCUSA's Siam Mission in 1860 and
helped to found the Petchaburi Station. In 1878, he
was appointed Superintendent of Public Instruction
and President of Royal College in Bangkok, the first
college opened in Siam. He remained in that position until his retirement in 1896.

McFarland's letterpress volume contains reports and
outgoing correspondence for the period 1876-1882.

19. Annual mission meeting at Lampang, Thailand, 1917.

UNITED STATES

MEXICO

Gulf of
Mexico

ATLANTIC

Mexico
City
Vera
Cruz
Merida
Campeche

Oaxaca

Quezaltenango
Guatemala
City

Barranquilla
Cartagena
Cúcuta

Caracas

VENEZUELA

Medellin   Bucaramanga

Bogotá

COLOMBIA

EQUATOR

ECUADOR

Amazon R.

PACIFIC

P E R U

B R A Z I L

Tocantins

BOLIVIA

Xingu

Araguaya

Francisco R.

Bomfim
Ponta Nova

Rosario Oeste

Bam Jesus
da Lapa   Caetetê

Burity

Lageado

São
Salvador
(Bahia)

Jatahy

São

Condeúba

Planaltina

OCEAN

Taltal

Beruery   Campinas

Castro   Rio de Janeiro
São Paulo

A R G E N T I N A

Paraná R.

Paraguay R.

Herval

Valparaiso Santiago
Curico
Concepción

Rio Lages

Uruguay R.   Capinzal

URUGUAY

Buenos
Aires

C H I L E

OCEAN

LATIN AMERICA
MISSIONS
THE BOARD OF FOREIGN MISSIONS
PRESBYTERIAN CHURCH, U. S. A.
156 FIFTH AVE. NEW YORK, N. Y.

LATIN AMERICA

Brazil

The PCUSA's Brazil Mission was established in 1859.
It was the second mission field opened by the PCUSA
in Latin America. The structure of the Brazil Mission differed from that of other fields developed
throughout the rest of Latin America. While the
latter evolved around permanent, centralized stations, few such stations were established in Brazil.
Due to the vast distances that had to be traveled by
itinerant missionaries, the Brazil Mission was subdivided in 1871 into two missions: the South Brazil
Mission and the Central Brazil Mission. The South
Brazil Mission included the stations in Sao Paulo,
Parana, Matto Grosso, Goyaz and Sante Catharina.
The Central Brazil Mission encompassed the stations
at Bahia, Cidade de Bomfim, Ponte Nova, Coetete and
North Minas. In 1938, the two missions were merged
and known as the Central Brazil Mission.

Southern Presbyterians, led by George Nash Morton
and Edward Lane, began their mission work in south
Brazil at Campinas in 1869. PCUS work centered
around Lauras in Minas Gerais and Mato Grosso (East
Brazil Mission); Goyas (West Brazil Mission); and in
the territory from the states north of Bahia to the
mouth of the Amazon River (North Brazil Mission).

The PCUSA's work in Brazil was evangelistic, educational and medical in nature. Though permanent institutions were constructed in the cities, evangelistic work in the interior was directed by itinerant
missionaries. In the South Brazil Mission, educational work centered in Sao Paulo, where primary,
intermediate and secondary education courses were
taught in Escolo Americana and higher education

provided at Mackenzie College. In the Central Brazil Mission, the Farm School of Ponte Nova offered
coeducational training. The only medical work of
the Central Brazil Mission was conducted at the
Ponte Nova Hospital.

The PCUSA encouraged the establishment of an indi-
genuous church in Brazil. In 1888, the churches
that had been formed by the missions of the PCUSA
and the PCUS united to form the Presbyterian Church
of Brazil, encompassing some fifty-two churches and
four presbyteries. The first General Assembly met
in 1910. A growing divergence of opinion on matters
of doctrine, policy, and methods however resulted in
a schism in 1903, causing a number of ministers, elders, and communicants to withdraw from the national
church and to establish their own Independent Presbyterian Church.

* * * * *

72. BOARD OF FOREIGN MISSIONS (PCUSA/UPCUSA), RE-
    CORDS, SECRETARIES' FILES, BRAZIL MISSION,
    1859-1972, [MF 24 R., 1859-1911; 1890-1972, 15
    FT., RG 86/137]

The PCUSA's educational, evangelistic and medical
work is documented in the Brazil Mission Secretaries' Files, 1859-1972. The microfilmed material
consists of outgoing/incoming correspondence, 1859-
1911, except for the period 1874-1878. Record
groups 86 and 137 consists of minutes, reports and
correspondence from the South and Central Brazil
Mission and its successor, the Central Brazil Mission, 1890-1972.

Arrangement of RG 86: Series I. South/Central Brazil Missions, 1911-1965; Series II. Mackenzie College, 1890-1961; Series III. Miscellany, 1902-1955.

Arrangement of RG 137: Series I. Minutes, reports
and correspondence, 1956-1972.

Chile

Protestant missionary efforts in Chile commenced in
1845 with the arrival in Valparaiso of David Trumbull. Sponsored by the Seamen's Friends Society and
the American Foreign Christian Union, Trumbull organized the Union Church for English-speaking Prot-
Protestants in 1847. In 1873, the work in Chile was
transferred to the PCUSA's Board of Foreign Missions, with that body assuming responsibility for
Trumbull and the other missionaries in the field.
Chile was the third field in Latin America occupied
by PCUSA missionaries.

Valparaiso and Santiago were established as mission
stations in 1868. Taltal was organized in northern
Chile in 1888, followed by Concepcion a decade later. Curico, the last station, was established in
1912. The work of the PCUSA in Chile was primarily
evangelistic and educational in nature. Schools
such as Escuela Popular, the Instituto Ingles, the
Union Bible Seminary and the Woman's Union Training
School testify to the church's concern for the educational needs of the Chilean people. The limited
medical work conducted by the PCUSA was done so at
institutions like the Madre e Hijo Hospital and the
San Martin Baby Dispensary.

In 1947, the Chile Mission requested dissolution by
the Board of Foreign Missions and that all its responsibilities be assumed by the Presbyterian Church
of Chile, the indigenous Chile church. The following year, a plan of administration was established
to implement this transfer. In 1950, a ten year
program was adopted that would gradually result in
the withdrawal of all fraternal workers with a

corresponding reduction of funds contributed by the
PCUSA. In 1962, the Presbyterian Church of Chile,
which is one of six Presbyterian denominations in
the country, became an autonomous church. Despite
this, however, it still conducts mission projects in
cooperation with Presbyterians in the United States.

* * * * *

73. BOARD OF FOREIGN MISSIONS, (PCUSA/UPCUSA), RE-
    CORDS, SECRETARIES' FILES, CHILE MISSION, 1866-
    1972, [MF 12 R.,1872-1911; 1866-1972, 10 FT., RG
    160]

The Secretaries' Files for the Chile Mission document the evangelistic and educational work of the
PCUSA/UPCUSA, 1866-1972. The microfilmed material
consists of outgoing/incoming correspondence, minutes and reports, 1872-1911. Record group 160
consists of similar materials, 1866-1972, though the
bulk of the materials date from 1911 through 1955.

Arrangement: Series I. Minutes, 1911-1962; Series II. Reports, 1910-1959; Series III. Correspondence, 1898-1972; Series IV. Mission Treasurer,
1926-1968; Series V. Property, 1866-1957; Series VI.
Miscellany, 1888-1967.

Colombia

Presbyterian work in Colombia began in 1856 when
Rev. Horace B. Pratt was sent by the PCUSA to establish a mission station in Bogota. Initially,
favorable conditions for evangelization existed, but
civil war and staunch opposition from the government
and the Roman Catholic Church precluded further expansion. For the next thirty-two years, Bogota remained the center of the PCUSA's work in Colombia.
Subsequent stations were later established at Barranquilla (1888), Medellin (1889), Bucaramanga
(1912), Cerete (1913), Cartagena (1914), and Ocana
(1934). Representatives of the Cumberland Presbyterian Church commenced mission work in Colombia in
1926 in the city of Cali. Subsequent work was
established by that church in the cities of Pereira,
Armenia and Cartago.

Though Colombia was the first Latin American country
occupied by Presbyterian missionaries, progress
there was remarkably slow compared to other Latin
American fields. Poor communication facilities en-
hanced the mission's isolation, though by the 1930s
and 1940s expanded air travel mitigated this some-
what. Resistance to Protestant work was intense
from the overwhelmingly large Roman Catholic population, from the hierarchy of the Roman Catholic
Church and from the government. The election of
liberal President Herrera in 1930 signaled a more
favorable attitude toward Protestants that resulted
in the adoption of the 1936 constitution, guaran-
teeing religious freedom to all Christians. In
1937, the Presbyterian Church of Colombia was organized and two years later, the Colombia Synod
procured a charter from the Synod Holding Corpo-

ration, thereby insuring the Synod's ability to hold
title to its property - an important step in stabi-
lizing the Protestant presence in Colombia.

The liberalization of the 1930s and the advent of
the Second World War did much to encourage the expansion of the PCUSA's work in Colombia. Displaced
missionaries from the Orient were transferred to
Colombia and for the first time in its history, the
Colombia Mission operated with a full staff. This
period of unprecedented growth was checked, however,
during the late 1940s. The return of civil war to
Colombia in 1948 and the subsequent triumph of the
Conservative Party marked a new era of Protestant
persecution. Though the more violent aspects of
this era had subsided by 1960, the crucial question
of the relationship between the Roman Catholic
Church and the Colombian government was at that time
still unresolved.

The PCUSA/UPCUSA's ministry in Colombia was primarily evangelistic and educational in nature, evi-
denced by the development of schools such as the
Colegio Americano for girls and boys in Bogota and
the Bible Training School in Medellin. In 1959,
Colombia's mission status formally ended when the
mission was integrated within the Colombian Presbyterian Church, though financial and personnel
support from the UPCUSA continued until the early
1970s.

                    * * * * *

74. BOARD OF FOREIGN MISSIONS (PCUSA/UPCUSA), RE-
    CORDS, SECRETARIES' FILES, COLOMBIA MISSION,
    1854-1972, [MF 24 R., 1854-1911; 1882-1972, 8
    V., 16 FT., RG 88]

The Secretaries' Files of the Colombia Mission evidence the educational and evangelistic work of the
PCUSA/UPCUSA, 1854-1972. The microfilmed materials
consist of outgoing and incoming correspondence,
1854-1911. Record group 88 consists of reports,
minutes, correspondence and miscellaneous materials,
1882-1972, though the bulk dates from 1911.

Arrangement: Series I. Reports, 1905-1971; Series
II. Minutes, 1912-1967; Series III. Correspondence,
1882-1972; Series IV. Miscellany, 1915-1972; Series
V. Mission History, 1917-1926; Series VI. Barranquilla Station Minutes, 1919-1944; Series VII. Cartagena Station Minutes, 1925-1927; Series VIII. Bo-

gota Station Minutes, 1923-1935; Series IX. Executive Committee Minutes, 1924-1957 and General Letters, 1943-1951.

75. BRADLEY, RUTH WINIFRED (1895-), PAPERS, 1923-1944, 1 FOL.

Ruth Winifred Bradley was appointed to the PCUSA's Colombia Mission in 1922. She taught and later served as vice-principal of the Girls' School in Barranquilla until her retirement from missionary service in 1960.

Her papers consist of miscellaneous correspondence and reports, 1923-1944.

20. Brazilian missionary the Reverend Alexander Blackford, circa 1888.

21. Guatemala missionaries Genevieve and Carl Malurstrom, [n.d.].

22. First meeting of the Mexican Synod, July 1901.

23. Mam Indian congregation in Guatemala, 1953.

24. Annual meeting of Mexico mission, Oaxaca, 1925.

Guatemala

Guatemala was the fifth field in Latin America to be
opened by Presbyterian missionaries. In 1882, the
Reverend and Mrs. John C. Hill of the PCUSA arrived
in Guatemala City at the request of and with financial support from the liberal government of Justo
Rufino Barrios. Guatemala City remained the only
mission station until 1898, when work was begun at
Quezaltenango despite considerable local opposition.

The PCUSA's work in Guatemala was evangelistic, educational and medical in nature. Though the mission
was limited to only two stations, it succeeded in
organizing a number of churches. In 1936, the Synod
of the Evangelical Church in Guatemala was formed,
incorporating the work of the PCUSA and four other
mission agencies. The PCUSA's educational work began in 1883, and resulted in the founding of several schools, notably, La Patria, a girls' school established in 1913 and the Norton Hall Industrial
School for Boys in 1929. Medical work was initiated
in 1906, followed by the opening of Hospital Americano at Guatemala City in 1913. Though Guatemala's
mission status ended in 1962 when the mission was
transferred to the Evangelical Presbyterian Church
of Guatemala, Presbyterian fraternal workers are
still operative in that field under the auspices of
the indigenous church.

* * * * *

76. BOARD OF FOREIGN MISSIONS (PCUSA/UPCUSA), RE-
    CORDS, SECRETARIES' FILES, GUATEMALA MISSION,
    1882-1972, [MF 7 R., 1882-1911; 1922-1972, 7
    FT., RG 157]

The Secretaries' Files for the Guatemala Mission reflect the PCUSA's evangelical, medical and educational work, 1882-1972. The microfilmed material
consists of outgoing correspondence and reports,
1882-1911. Record group 157 consists of similar
material and covers the period from 1911-1972.

Arrangement: Series I. Minutes, 1911-1971; Series
II. Reports, 1911-1972; Series III. Correspondence,
1911-1972.

77. BURGESS FAMILY PAPERS, 1904-1963, 8 FT., RG 201

Paul Burgess (1886-1958) and Dora McLaughlin Burgess
(1887-1962) were appointed to the PCUSA's Guatemala
Mission in 1912, serving there until their retirement in 1956. Until 1932, they served at Quezaltenango where they performed general evangelistic
work. Dora Burgess taught and served as principal
of La Patria while Paul Burgess served as pastor of
the Bethel Presbyterian Church. In 1932, they commenced a ministry to the Quiche Indians that included mastering the Quiche native language and
generating Christian literature in it. They were
responsible for establishing the Quiche Bible Institute, an ecumenical project that provided spiritual
training for the more than 300,000 Quiche Indians
living in Guatemala. In addition to their teaching
and evangelistic work, the Burgesses spent a prodi-
gious amount of time engaged in literary work that
encompassed a variety of subjects including, Christian socialism, political and church history, missionary work, folk lore, hymnology and theology.

The Burgess Family Papers consists of incoming and
outgoing correspondence, diaries, notebooks and
scrapbooks, 1904-1963 and documents the development
of Presbyterian mission work in Guatemala.

Arrangement: Series I. Correspondence, 1905-1963;
Series II. Diaries/Notebooks, 1904-1960; Series III.
Scrapbooks, circa 1904-1950s.

Mexico

The PCUSA was the first Protestant denomination to
initiate missionary work in Mexico. Though formally
commenced in 1872, the PCUSA had appointed Rev. and
Mrs. William C. Blair and Rev. Daniel Baker to the
newly independent Republic of Texas in 1839, as a
prelude to establishing mission work south of the
Rio Grande.

Until 1857, all forms of religion except Roman Ca-
tholicism were forbidden in Mexico. In that year,
legislation passed by liberal leader Benito Juarez
permitted freedom of worship and thus encouraged the
development of evangelical churches. Stirrings of
independent thought were manifested in many of the
northern towns and in Mexico City, resulting in the
establishment of Bible study groups under the direction of Arcadio Morales, T.F. Wallace, Maxwell Phil-
lips, C.C. Millar and Dr. J. Greene. When in 1872
the PCUSA General Assembly voted to establish a formal mission in Mexico, its foundation was based upon
the work of these earlier leaders.

The PCUSA was one of several Presbyterian denominations conducting missionary work in Mexico. The
PCUS established a mission in Mexico in 1874 when
Anthony Graybill started work at Matamoras in north-
eastern Mexico. Cumberland Presbyterians sent Rev.
A.H. Whatley to Mexico in 1886 to begin work at
Aguascalientes where four mission stations were established. Three additional stations were later
opened at Guanajuato.

The PCUSA's Mexico Mission, like others throughout
Latin America, operated on a decentralized basis.

Administratively, only two stations existed: Central Station, founded in 1972; and Peninsula Station, founded in 1915. Central Station included Vera Cruz (1897) and Oaxaca (1919) while the three states of Yucatan, Campeche, Tabasco and the territory of Quintana Roo comprised the Peninsula Station. Because of the uneven distribution of Protestant missionaries, a plan was devised in 1915 among the various denominations operative in Mexico to address this imbalance. As a result of the "Cincinnati Plan," the PCUSA surrendered its older established work in the states of Zacatecas, Guerrero and Michoacan. Southern Presbyterians moved to Central Mexico into the area formally occupied by the PCUSA, this new field being south and west of Mexico City.

Despite its legal status, Protestant mission work in Mexico was subject to persecution that was both religiously and politically inspired. Tension between the Mexican and U.S. governments consistently hindered the mission's work. Strife between various Mexican political factions together with the turmoil resultant from civil war and revolution further retarded the work of the mission. The Mexican Constitution of 1917 and the enactment of legislation during the 1930s limited Protestant influence in such areas as ordination of ministers, education and property ownership. Though private worship was not to be interfered with, public worship was only to be held in church buildings specifically recognized by the state.

Regardless of these restrictions, the PCUSA ministered to the educational and spiritual needs of the Mexican people. Though the mission did not engage in any regular medical work, it did conduct modest clinic work and shared in the training of nurses in the Baptist Hospital in Puebla and the Southern Presbyterian Hospital in Morelia. Schools were established in San Angel, later called Villa Obregon, Coyoacan and in the State of Oaxaca. Bible Training Schools flourished in the Federal District, in Oaxaca and in Merida, Yucatan, where the Turner-Hodge School for girls and boys attracted large numbers of students. Since the 1930s, the concept of Christian education has been increasingly difficult to implement given the rise of state supported secular schools and the constitutional restrictions on religious instruction.

The evangelical work of the mission, though limited in nature, was conducted among the military and with

students. Small congregations, initially served by
missionaries of the PCUSA, were eventually replaced
by Mexican evangelists trained in various Bible
schools. The first synod was established in 1904
and in 1947, the General Assembly of the Mexican
Presbyterian Church was organized. Since that time,
Presbyterian missionaries and later fraternal workers have cooperated with the Mexican Presbyterian
Church in theological, evangelical and other efforts.

* * * * *

78. BLACKBURN, EUNICE R. (1886-1981), PAPERS, 1920-
     1977, 1 FT., RG 198

Eunice R. Blackburn was appointed by the PCUSA to
the Mexico Mission in 1920. Until her retirement in
1951, she taught and later served as principal of
the Turner Hodge American School in Merida, Yucatan.

Eunice R. Blackburn's papers consist of incoming and
outgoing correspondence and miscellaneous items,
including scrapbooks, photographs, clippings and reports 1920-1977.

79. BOARD OF FOREIGN MISSIONS (PCUSA/UPCUSA), RE-
     CORDS, SECRETARIES' FILES, MEXICO MISSION, 1867-
     1972, [MF 18 R., 1872-1911; 1867-1972, 26 FT.,
     RG 87]

The Secretaries' Files of the Mexico Mission documents the PCUSA's educational and evangelistic work,
1867-1972. The microfilmed materials consists of
outgoing correspondence, reports and minutes, 1872-
1911. Record group 87 is comprised of minutes, reports and correspondence, 1867-1971, though the bulk
of the collection dates from 1911.

Arrangement: Series I. Minutes, 1911-1970; Series
II. Reports, 1896-1972; Series III. Correspondence,
1867-1972; Series IV. Mission Treasurer, 1884-1967;
Series V. Miscellany, 1904-1972.

Venezuela

Venezuela was the last mission field in Latin American to be occupied by the PCUSA. Work began in 1897 when Rev. and Mrs. T.S. Pond of the Colombia Mission were transferred to Caracas. Despite considerable prejudice towards Protestants, a church was established there in 1900 and the station was formally organized as a separate mission in 1912. The work of the PCUSA was limited chiefly to Caracas in the Federal District and in the neighboring state of Miranda.

The mission's work in Venezuela was primarily educational and evangelistic in nature. Educational work commenced in 1900 with the establishment of Colegio Americana, a school for girls and young women. Other educational facilities were later established at Guatire (Primary School) and Ocumare (Christian Rural Center). Evangelistic work was mainly restricted to Caracas, the only mission station.

In 1945, the Presbytery of Venezuela was organized, though the number of communicants in the Presbyterian Church of Venezuela was and continued to be small amidst an overwhelmingly Roman Catholic population. In 1961, the Venezuela Mission was formally dissolved, with its work being assumed by the Presbyterian Church of Venezuela.

* * * * *

80. BOARD OF FOREIGN MISSIONS (PCUSA/UPCUSA) RE-
    CORDS, SECRETARIES' FILES, VENEZUELA MISSION,
    1897-1972, [MF 4 R., 1897-1911; 1911-1972, 4
    FT, RG. 99]

The Secretaries' Files of the Venezuela Mission reflect the educational and evangelistic work of the
PCUSA/UPCUSA, 1897-1972. The microfilmed material
consists of outgoing correspondence, 1897-1911. Record group 99 consists of correspondence, minutes,
reports and miscellaneous items, 1911-1972.

Arrangement: Series I. Correspondence, 1911-1972;
Series II. Minutes, 1923-1972; Series III. Reports,
1919-1970; Series IV. Miscellany, 1917-1971.

**81. VENEZUELA MISSION (PCUSA/UPCUSA), RECORDS,
    1897-1966, 3 FT., RG 159**

Record group 159 consists of the records maintained
by the Venezuela Mission, 1897-1966.

Arrangement: Series I. Minutes, 1913-1961; Series
II. Reports, 1897-1960; Series III. Correspondence,
1897-1966; Series IV. Miscellany, 1927-1966.

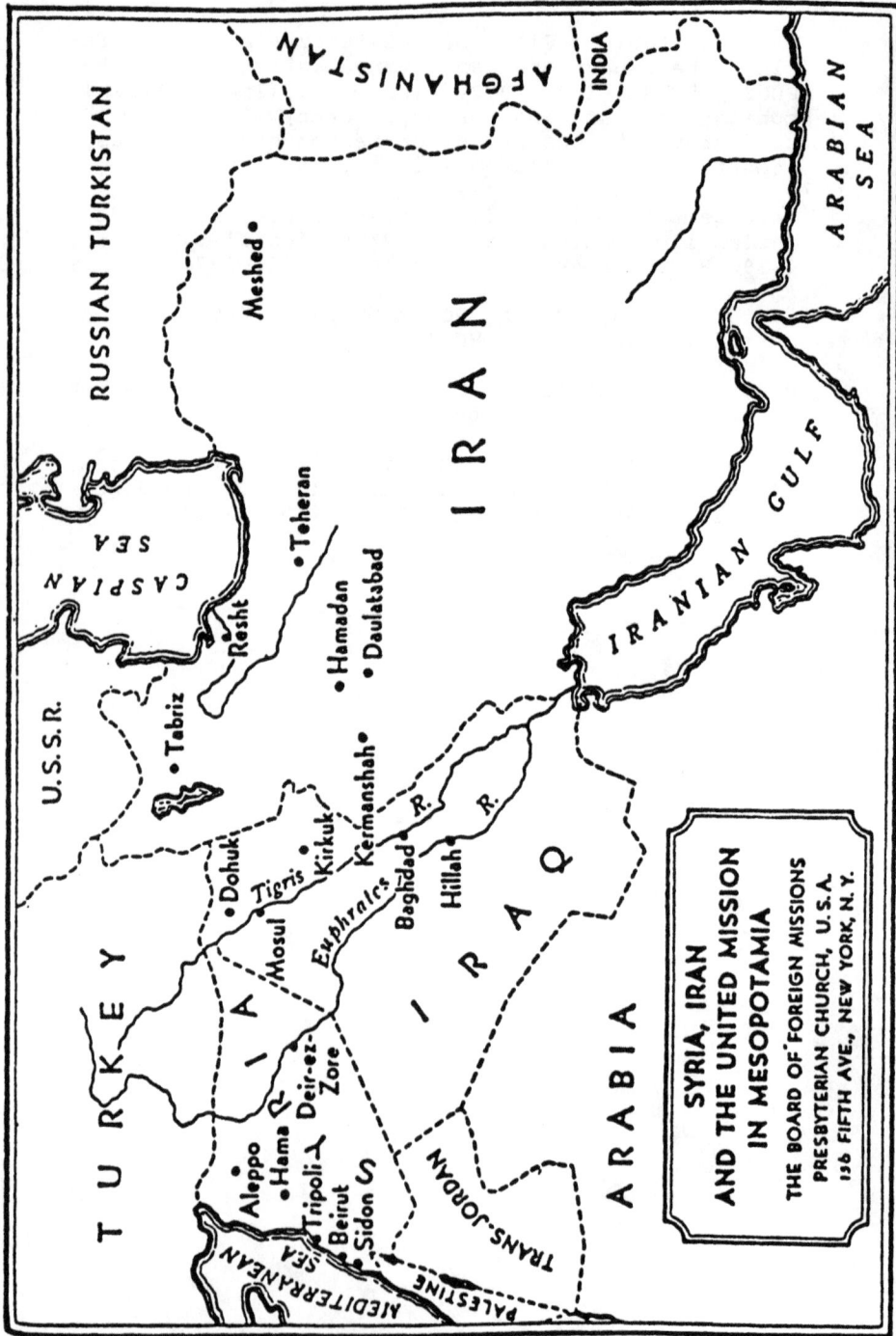

SYRIA, IRAN
AND THE UNITED MISSION
IN MESOPOTAMIA

THE BOARD OF FOREIGN MISSIONS
PRESBYTERIAN CHURCH, U.S.A.
156 FIFTH AVE., NEW YORK, N.Y.

MIDDLE EAST

Iran (Persia)

American Protestant missionary efforts in Persia began in 1829 when Eli Smith and Timothy Dwight were
sent by the ABCFM to explore the regions of north-
western Persia. Upon their recommendation, the
ABCFM established a mission to the Nestorian Christians at Urumia in 1834 and appointed Justin Perkins
as its first missionary. In 1871, the ABCFM's Mission to Persia was transferred to the PCUSA, thus
formally commencing Presbyterian work in Persia.
Within a decade the PCUSA's Persia Mission had expanded to include new stations at Teheran (1872),
Urumia (1873), Tabriz (1873) and Hamadan (1880).
Due to the vast differences between stations, the
Persia Mission was divided in 1883 with Urumia and
Tabriz organized as the West Persia Mission while
Hamadan and Teheran constituted the East Persia
Mission. The latter was later to include the new
stations of Resht and Kazvin (1906), Kermanshah
(1910) and Meshed (1911). The East and West Persia
Missions were later reunited in 1931 and were known
as the Persia, and after 1935, the Iran Mission.

The PCUSA's work in Persia was evangelical, educational and medical in nature. Numerous local congregations were organized and eventually served by
native ministers of the Central Evangelical Church
of Iran, organized in 1934. Medical work began as
early as 1835 and progressed during the latter half
of the nineteenth century. Formal hospitals were
built in Kermanshah (1882), Teheran (1890) and
Tabriz (1913) with similar institutions established
in Meshed, Hamadan and Resht. Numerous schools were

established, many of which developed into multina-
tional institutions such as the Alborz Foundation
(Armaghan Institute), Iran Bethel (Damavand)
College, the Community School of Teheran and the
Mehr Jordan Schools.

The Iran Mission was formally dissolved in 1960.
Since then, the UPCUSA has worked with the Evangelical Church of Iran, providing both personnel and
financial support requisite to maintain certain
medical and educational institutions.

* * * * *

82. BOARD OF FOREIGN MISSIONS (PCUSA/UPCUSA), RE-
     CORDS, SECRETARIES FILES, IRAN MISSION, 1847-
     1973, [MF 25 R., 1847-1910; 1881-1968, 25 FT.,
     RG 91; 1956-1973, 3 FT., RG 161; 32 V.]

The Iran Mission's Secretaries' Files documents the
PCUSA/UPCUSA educational, evangelistic and medical
work, 1847-1973. The microfilmed material consists
of outgoing and incoming correspondence, minutes,
reports and miscellaneous items, 1847-1910. Record
group 91 consists of similar materials, 1881-1968,
though its bulk dates from 1911. Record Group 161
documents the declining years of the Iran Mission,
1956-1973, and consists of minutes, correspondence
and reports.

Arrangement of RG 91: Series I. East Persia Mission, 1911-1930; Series II. West Persia Mission,
1911-1930; Series III. Persia and Iran Mission,
1931-1968; Series IV. Mission Secretary, 1911-1965;
Series V. Alborz College, 1908-1966; Series VI. Miscellaneous Correspondence, 1881-1937; Series VII.
Station Files, 1911-1968; Hamadan Station Record
Book of Language Students, 1945-1960; Minutes of
East Persia Mission, 1882-1911; Tabriz Station,
Tabriz Protestant Girls' School, 1879-1928; Minutes
of the Teheran Station, 1925-1942; 1945-1951; 1953-
1964; Minutes of the Urumia Mission, 1919-1929;
1931-1934; Series VIII. Miscellany, 1900-1966.

Arrangement of RG 161: Series I. Correspondence,
1956-1973; Series II. Minutes/reports, 1956-1972;
Series III. Miscellany, 1956-1970; Series IV. Institutional files, 1956-1972.

83. DOUGLAS, CHARLES A. (1871-1918), PAPERS, 1901-
    1916, 5 V.

Charles A. Douglas was appointed to the PCUSA's East
Persia Mission in 1901. He performed evangelistic
work and served as Mission Secretary and Treasurer
until his death on the field of typhoid in 1918.

Douglas' papers consists of diaries, 1904-1916 (3
v.) and correspondence, 1901-1908 (2 v.).

84. ELDER FAMILY PAPERS, 1925-1979, .5 FT., RG 189

John Elder (1894-1983) and Ruth Roche Elder (1899-)
were assigned to the PCUSA's East Persia Mission in
1921. They performed evangelistic work in Kermanshah (1923-1934), Hamadan (1934-1937) and Teheran
(1938-1964). Rev. Elder served as pastor of the
Persian speaking congregation in each city. In
1935, he was elected Moderator of the newly formed
Eastern Presbytery of Iran and also served as Moderator of the Synod of Iran in 1947 and 1960. The
Elders retired from missionary service in 1964.

The Elder Family Papers consists of John and Ruth
Roche Elder's correspondence, reports, photographs
and miscellaneous items, 1925-1979.

Arrangement: Series I. John Elder, 1925-1979; Series II. Ruth Roche Elder, 1927-1960; Series III.
Photographs, 1923-1970s; Series IV. Miscellany,
1920s-1970s.

**85. HAWKES, SARAH BELLE SHERWOOD (1854-1919), PA-
PERS, 1872-1919, 1 FT., RG 116**

Sarah Belle Sherwood was appointed to the PCUSA's
East Persia Mission in 1883. In 1884, she married
the Reverend James W. Hawkes also of the East Persia
Mission. Her entire career was spent at Hamadan
where she taught and performed evangelistic work
with Armenian, Jewish and Moslem women and children. She died in service in 1919.

Sarah Belle Sherwood Hawkes' papers consist of correspondence to family, diaries, photographs and miscellaneous items, 1872-1919.

**86. HOLLIDAY, MARGARET YANDES (1843-1920), JOURNAL,
1906, 1 V.**

Margaret Yandes Holliday was appointed in 1883 to
the PCUSA's West Persia Mission. She served at
Tabriz where she was engaged in evangelistic work.
Following the Turkish invasion of Tabriz in 1918,

she went to Kasvin where she continued her evangel-
itic work with women and children. Ill health necessitated her return to the U.S. in 1919 where she
died in 1920.

Margaret Yandes Holliday's journal, dated 1906, consists of unpublished narratives about Moslem con-
verts to Christianity.

87. IRWIN FAMILY PAPERS, (1932-1965), 1 FT., RG 205

Reverend John Mark Irwin (1899-) and Ruth Hoffman
Irwin (1900-) were appointed to the PCUSA's Persia
Mission in 1932. Until their retirement in 1965,
they served mainly as evangelists at various loca-
tions in Iran, including Meshed, Hamadan, and Sari,
as well as in Kabul, Afghanistan.

The Irwin Family Papers consist almost exclusively
of personal correspondence from Ruth Hoffman Irwin,
1932-1965. Limited correspondence from J. Mark Irwin can also be found for the years 1932-1939.

Arrangement: Series I. Correspondence, 1932-1965;
Series II. Miscellany, 1930s-1960s.

25. Leree Stella Chase, circa 1964.

26. Belle Sherwood Hawkes, circa 1885.

27. Annual mission meeting, Teheran, Persia [Iran], 1902.

Iraq (Mesopotamia)

Protestant work in Mesopotamia dates from 1834 when
the ABCFM sent Justin Perkins to labor among the
Nestorian Christians. For the next thirty years,
missionaries ministered to this group and to the
Kurds in the mountainous areas between Urumia and
Mosul. In 1870, the ABCFM's work in these areas was
transferred to the PCUSA. Urumia became part of the
West Persia Mission in 1873, followed by Mosul in
1891. The latter, however, was transferred to the
Church Missionary Society in 1900.

The upheaval resultant from the First World War precluded the Church Missionary Society from resuming
its prewar responsibilities in Mesopotamia. Short
of a complete withdrawal from this field, it was de-
cided to transfer the work to the various American
mission groups that had been operative there before
1900. Thus out of the problems of adjustment, reorganization and depleted staffs arose the idea of a
United Mission in Mesopotamia. Initially, the plan
was to include in one mission all of the Presbyte-
rian/Reformed churches. The plan as actually adopted in 1924 included the PCUSA, the Reformed Church
in America and the Reformed Church in the United
States. In 1935, the name of the mission was
changed to the United Mission in Iraq. Following
denominational reorganizations in the 1950s and
1960s, representatives of the Reformed Church in
America, the PCUS, the United Church of Christ and
the UPCUSA constituted the United Mission. Govern-
ance was through a Joint Committee headquartered in
New York.

The work of the United Mission centered around five
stations, three of which were staffed by Presbyterian personnel. These included: Mosul, the center
of the old West Persia Mission; Hillah, occupied as
an out station in 1926 and elevated to a full
station in 1930; and Dohuk occupied in 1930. Work
in Baghdad was directed by the Reformed Church in
America while the Reformed Church in the United
States operated in Kirkuk. The primary focus of the
Mission's work was educational with schools being
established in Baghdad and Mosul. By the early
1960s, all of the evangelical groups operative in
Iraq were part of the United Mission, though an
indigenous church did not yet exist. Early in 1970,
the Mission's two schools were seized by the Iraqi
government, causing the Joint Committee to indefi-
nitely suspend all of its activities. On June 30,
1970, the United Mission in Iraq and its governing
body were formally dissolved.

* * * * *

**88. BOARD OF FOREIGN MISSIONS (PCUSA/UPCUSA), RE-
    CORDS, 1924-1970, 2 FT., RG 89**

Record group 89 consists of the records of the United Mission in Mesopotamia/Iraq, 1924-1971. Included are minutes, correspondence and reports that reflect the history, organization and activities of
the United Mission.

Syria/Lebanon

American Protestant mission work in Syria-Lebanon
dates from 1819 when Pliny Fisk and Levi Parsons
under the ABCFM arrived in Smyrna to begin a ministry in the Jerusalem area. In 1870, the ABCFM's
mission to Syria-Lebanon was transferred to the
PCUSA.

The work of the PCUSA in Syria-Lebanon was conducted
at four main stations, three of which were inherited
from the ABCFM. These included Beirut, occupied in
1823; Tripoli, opened in 1848; and Sidon, occupied
in 1851. The last station, Aleppo, was opened by
the PCUSA in 1920. Besides these four stations and
their sixty-three outstations, several substations
also existed. Suk-el-Gharb, established by the
ABCFM in 1848, became part of Beirut as did Zahleh.
Hama and Deir-ez-Zore were both substations of Aleppo. The work of the Syria Mission transcended three
states: Lebanon, which encompassed the stations of
Beirut, Tripoli, Sidon and the substation of Zahleh;
Latakia, where limited evangelism work was performed
in certain villages; and Syria, where work was conducted in the cities of Hama, Aleppo and Deir-ez-
Zore.

The conflict between Christian and Moslem, a domi-
nant and reoccurring theme throughout the area's
history, presented the Mission with a diversity of
problems unknown in many other mission fields. The
division of the population along religious lines resulted in internecine warfare throughout the country
and had an unsettling effect on the Mission's educational, medical and evangelistic work. Despite the
turmoil, progress was achieved, especially in the

areas of educational and medical work. Institutions
like the American School for Girls, the Syrian Protestant College (later known as the American University of Beirut), the Tripoli Girls School and the
Gerald Institute illustrate the PCUSA's commitment
to education. Medical work was carried on in three
centers: the Hamlin Memorial Sanitarium for tuber-
cular patients; the Kennedy Memorial Hospital in
Tripoli; and the Deir-ez-Zore Hospital in the remote
northern desert.

The first evangelical church in Syria-Lebanon was
organized in Beirut in 1848 and by 1921, the exist-
int three presbyteries united to form a synod.
Though a Syrian Evangelical Church was organized,
its communicants were few in number. In 1959, the
American Presbyterian Mission in Syria-Lebanon was
dissolved and its work integrated into the National
Evangelical Synod of Syria and Lebanon.

* * * * *

89. BOARD OF FOREIGN MISSIONS (PCUSA/UPCUSA), RE-
    CORDS, SECRETARIES' FILES, SYRIA-LEBANON MIS-
    SION, 1836-1972, [MF 20 R.,1869-1910; 1836-1972,
    15.5 FT., RG 90, 16 V.]

The Secretaries' Files for the Syria-Lebanon Mission
documents the work of the PCUSA/UPCUSA, 1869-1972.
The microfilmed materials consists of outgoing and
incoming correspondence, minutes and reports, 1869-
1910. Record group 90 consists of similar materials, though the bulk of the collection dates from
1911-1972.

Arrangement: Series I. Minutes, 1911-1970; Series
II. Reports, 1903-1972; Series III. Correspondence,
1911-1972; Series IV. Miscellany, 1894-1971; Series
V. American Community School Ledgers, 1908-1911;
Beirut Station Account Book, 1910-1915; Evangelical
Alliance Correspondence, 1873- 1876; Lebanon Sana-
torium Ledger, 1913-1916; Series VI. Sidon and Has-
beiya Station Records, 1851-1852; Sidon Station
Bookkeeper's Journal, 1920-1933; Tripoli Station
Records, 1848- 1896; Series VII. BFM Correspondence
to Syria Mission, 1870-1890; BFM Minutes, 1836-1838;
1870-1930; 1947-1950.

90. BOYES, FLORENCE RAY (1889-1972), PAPERS, 1953-
    1955, 1 FOL.

Florence Ray Boyes was appointed to the PCUSA's

Syria Mission in 1919 with her husband Henry Robert
Boyes, M.D. They served at Kennedy Memorial Hospital in Tripoli until their retirement in 1958.

Florence Ray Boyes' papers contain miscellaneous
correspondence and newsletters, 1953-1955.

91. IRWIN, FRANCES PRYOR (1895-1939), PAPERS, 1922-1935, 1 FT., RG 186

France Pryor Irwin was appointed to the PCUSA's
Syria Mission in 1921 and taught at the American
School for Girls in Beirut. In 1924, she was appointed principal of the newly formed American Junior College for Women and remained in that position
until her resignation from missionary service in
1937.

Arrangement: Series I. Correspondence, 1922-1935;
Series II. Photographs, 1922-1934.

92. JESSUP, HENRY HARRIS (1832-1910), PAPERS, 1853-1910, 2 FT., RG 183

Henry Harris Jessup was appointed as a missionary to
Syria in 1855 by the ABCFM and continued to serve
there following the transfer of the mission to the
PCUSA in 1870. Until 1860, Jessup resided in Tripoli with his family but spent the remainder of his
missionary service in Beirut where for thirty years
he was acting pastor of the Syrian Church of Beirut
and superintendent of its school. He served as the
secretary of the Asfuriyeh Hospital for the Insane
and as missionary editor of the Arabic journal,
El-Neshrah. Jessup was also one of the founders of
the Syrian Protestant College in Beirut. He died in
service in 1910 and was buried in Beirut.

Arrangement: Series I. Letterpress Correspondence,
1861-1900; Series II. Memoirs (unpublished and written ca. 1908- 1910), 1832-1908; Series III. Miscellany, 1853-1910.

93. SHANNON, WINIFRED (1900-1975), PAPERS, 1924-1950, 1 FT., RG 165

Winifred Shannon was appointed to the PCUSA's Syria
Mission in 1925 and was assigned to the American
Junior College for Women. From 1937 until 1941, she
was assigned to the Iran Mission's Sage College in
Teheran. From 1941-1944, she taught at the Isabella
Thoburn College in Lucknow, India. She retired from

mission service in 1952.

Arrangement: Series I. Diaries, Correspondence, Reports and Miscellany, 1924-1950.

94. STOLTZFUS, WILLIAM A. (1891-1964), PAPERS, 1920-
    1963, .5 FT, RG 166

William A. Stoltzfus was assigned to the PCUSA's
Syria Mission in 1921 and served as a teacher at Na-
batiyah, Suk-el-Gharb, and Tripoli. He was appointed principal of the North Syria Schools in 1932. In
1937, he was designated president of the American
Junior College for Women where he served until 1958.
Until his death in 1964, Stoltzfus served as Secretary for College Relations for Beirut College.

Arrangement: Series I. Correspondence/Reports,
1920-1963; Series II. Sermons/Addresses, 1933-1961.

95. SYRIA MISSION ARCHIVES, RECORDS, 1810-1967,
    20 FT., RG 115

Record group 115 consists of the records of the
Syria Mission Archives, 1808-1967, though the bulk
of the collection dates from 1823-1959. It includes
correspondence from missionaries and representatives
of the ABCFM, the PCUSA's Board of Foreign Missions
and its successor, as well as American, European and
Syrian government officials.

28. Henry Harris Jessup, Syrian missionary, [n.d.].

29. Dr. Mary Pierson Eddy of the Syria-Lebanon mission, [n.d.].

30. Frances Irwin Pryor and Syrian girl scouts, 1925.

31. Winifred Shannon and friend, [n.d.].

32. Arthur Judson Brown, secretary of the Board of Foreign Missions, 1895-1929, [n.d.].

Walter Lowrie

33. Walter Lowrie, secretary of the Board of Foreign Missions, 1837-1868, [n.d.].

34. Edward M. Dodd, M.D., medical secretary, of the Board of Foreign Missions, 1921-1957, [n.d.].

35. John Lowrie, assistant and coordinate secretary of the Board of Foreign Missions, 1838-1891, [n.d.].

Related Collections

* * * * *

96. AMERICAN BOARD OF COMMISSIONERS FOR FOREIGN MIS-
    SIONS, RECORDS, 1843-1854; 1851-1870, 2 V.

These records consists of two volumes of treasurer's
records, 1843-1870.

97. ASSOCIATE REFORMED CHURCH IN NORTH AMERICA, RE-
    CORDS, 1850-1856, 1 V.

These records consist of Board of Foreign Missions
minutes from the Associate Reformed Church in North
America, 1850-1856.

98. ASSOCIATE SYNOD OF NORTH AMERICA, RECORDS, 1844-
    1858, 1 V.

These records consist of Board of Foreign Mission
minutes from the Associate Synod of North America,
1844-1858.

99. CALVINISTIC METHODIST CHURCH IN THE U.S.A., RE-
    CORDS, 1904-1911, 1 FOL.

These records consist of the minutes of the Board of
Home and Foreign Missions of the Calvinistic Methodist Church in the U.S.A, 1904-1911.

100. CUMBERLAND PRESBYTERIAN CHURCH, RECORDS, 1847-
     1893, 3 V.

These records consist of the Cumberland Presbyterian
Church's Board of Foreign and Domestic Missions annual reports, 1847-1856; minutes, 1877-1893; and

miscellaneous records, 1869-1874.

101. LOWRIE, JOHN CAMERON (1808-1900), PAPERS, 1845-1885, .5 FT., RG 175

John Cameron Lowrie was appointed as a missionary to
India in 1833 by the Western Foreign Missionary Society. He served in Ludhiana until ill health com-
pelled his return to the U.S. in 1836. In 1838,
Lowrie was elected Assistant Corresponding Secretary
of the PCUSA's newly formed Board of Foreign Missions. In 1850, he became Corresponding Secretary
along with his father, Walter Lowrie, and served in
this position until his retirement in 1891.

Arrangement: Series I. Correspondence and reports,
1845-1885.

102. LOWRIE, WALTER (1784-1868), PAPERS, 1839-1871, 1 FT., RG 174

Walter Lowrie succeeded Elisha Swift in 1837 as Corresponding Secretary of the Western Foreign Society
and its successor, the Board of Foreign Missions.
Prior to his service with the PCUSA, Lowrie served
in the Pennsylvania Assembly (1811-1812); the State
Senate (1813-1819); and in the U.S. Senate (1819-
1825). In 1825, Lowrie was elected Secretary of
that body, a position that he held until 1836.

During his thirty-two year tenure as Corresponding
Secretary, the Board of Foreign Missions grew from
obscurity to an extensive missionary operation. He
solicited contributions for the Board and maintained
close touch with all phases of mission work. His
senatorial experience provided him a unique and de-
tailed knowledge of the needs of Native Americans
and he frequently visited these missions. In the
area of foreign missions, he corresponded extensively with those serving in Africa, India and China
as well as those ministering to the Native, Oriental
and Jewish Americans.

Arrangement: Series I. Correspondence and reports,
1839-1871 (including letterpress correspondence of
John Lowrie).

103. PRESBYTERIAN CHURCH IN THE U.S.A., SECRETARIES' FILES, MEDICAL DEPARTMENT, 1921-1961, 5 FT., RG 144

Established in 1921, the Medical Department was the

first organized attempt by the PCUSA's Board of Foreign Missions to supervise the health of missionaries on the foreign field. The PCUSA was one of
two Protestant denominations in this country to pio-
neer in the field of organized medical mission work.

The establishment of the Medical Department resulted
from the growing number of missionaries subject to
unsanitary conditions, malignant diseases and other
stresses that could impair their usefulness or
threaten their lives. In 1921, Edward M. Dodd,
M.D., a former missionary to Persia, was appointed
Acting Secretary and later Executive Secretary of
the Medical Department. The Department supervised
the health of mission personnel on furlough and in
the field and aided in the selection of missionary
candidates. It assisted in the recruitment of medical candidates and served as a liaison with medical
missionaries working in the field.

Record group 144 documents the broad range of interest and activity in medical missions, 1921-1961,
of the principal departmental correspondents, Drs.
E.M. Dodd and W.J.K. Clothier, Medical and Assistant
Medical Secretary respectively.

Arrangement: Series I. Medical Council/Committee,
1947-1957; Series II. Medical Department, 1926-
1959; Series III. Missionary Candidates Files,
1939-1956; Series IV. Foreign Students and Visiting
Nationals, 1937-1951; Series V. Miscellany,1927-
1956; Series VI. Missionary correspondence, 1923-
1960; Series VII. Mission Institutions, 1937-1959;
Series VIII. Subject Files, 1924-1961; Series IX.
Medical Education, 1925-1960; Series X. Sanitaria,
1921-1961.

104. PRESBYTERIAN CHURCH IN THE U.S.A., RECORDS,
     1837-1958, 108 V, .5 FT.

This collection consists of miscellaneous records
from the Board of Foreign Mission. Included are:
BFM Minutes, 1837-1958; Corporation Records and Mi-
nutes, 1852-1888; Missionary Records, 1872-1908;
Executive Committee Minutes, 1872-1908; Executive
Council Minutes, 1894-1905; 1908-1910; 1922-1958;
1937-1941; Correspondence regarding South America
Missions, 1878-1886.

105. PRESBYTERIAN CHURCH IN THE U.S.A./UNITED PRES-
     BYTERIAN CHURCH IN THE U.S.A., SECRETARIES'
     SUBJECT FILES, 1829-1965, 99 FT., RG 31/81

The Board of Foreign Missions Secretaries' Subject
Files contain primarily correspondence dealing with
foreign and domestic missions, 1829-1965. Record
group 31 consists of incoming correspondence to the
Secretaries and Treasurers of the Western Foreign
Missionary Society and its successor, the Board of
Foreign Missions, 1829-1895. It also contains minutes, reports and financial records relating to the
activities of the Board, its various committees and
its nineteenth century mission fields. Record group
81 contains minutes, correspondence and reports,
1892-1965, pertaining to the twentieth century mission fields where the PCUSA and the UPCUSA were
operative.

106. PRESBYTERIAN CHURCH IN THE U.S.A., WOMEN'S
     BOARD OF FOREIGN MISSIONS, RECORDS, 1876-1923,
     30 V., .5 FT., MF 5 R.

The records of the Women's Board of Foreign Missions
(WBFM) includes: Minutes and Reports of the Central
Committee, 1884-1920; Minutes of WBFM, 1884-1910;
Minutes of the Executive Committee, 1883-1912; Minutes of the Manager's Meetings, 1876-1914; Records
of Prayer Meetings, 1888-1903; Annual Reports,
1871-1923; Miscellaneous Records, 1876-1914.

107. UNITED PRESBYTERIAN CHURCH OF NORTH AMERICA,
     RECORDS, 1855-1859, 29 V.

The records of the UPCNA's Board of Foreign Missions
include: Financial Agents Records, 1855-1865; Executive Committee Minutes, 1948-1950; Minutes, 1859-
1958. Also included are the Minutes of the Women's
General Missionary Society (WGMS), 1884-1958; WGMS
Board of Director's Minutes, 1886-1959; and WGMS Financial Records, 1886-1888.

108. WESTERN FOREIGN MISSIONARY SOCIETY, RECORDS,
     1831-1837, 1 V., MF 1 R.

These records consist of minutes of the Western Foreign Missionary Society, 1831-1837 and annual reports, 1833-1837.

109. WOMAN'S NORTH PACIFIC PRESBYTERIAN BOARD OF
     MISSIONS, RECORDS, 1887-1920, 15 V.

These records include annual reports, 1889-1920 and
minutes, 1887-1920.

110. WOMAN'S PRESBYTERIAN BOARD OF MISSIONS OF THE
     NORTHWEST, RECORDS, 1883-1920, 1 V.

These records include minutes and reports, 1883-
1920.

111. WOMAN'S PRESBYTERIAN BOARD OF MISSIONS OF THE
     SOUTHWEST, RECORDS, 1883-1920, 4 V.

These records include annual reports, 1883-1920.

112. WOMAN'S PRESBYTERIAN FOREIGN MISSIONARY SOCIETY
     OF NORTHERN NEW YORK, RECORDS, 1872-1908, 4 V.

 These records includes annual reports, 1872-1908.

Appendix:
The Presbyterian Family Connection

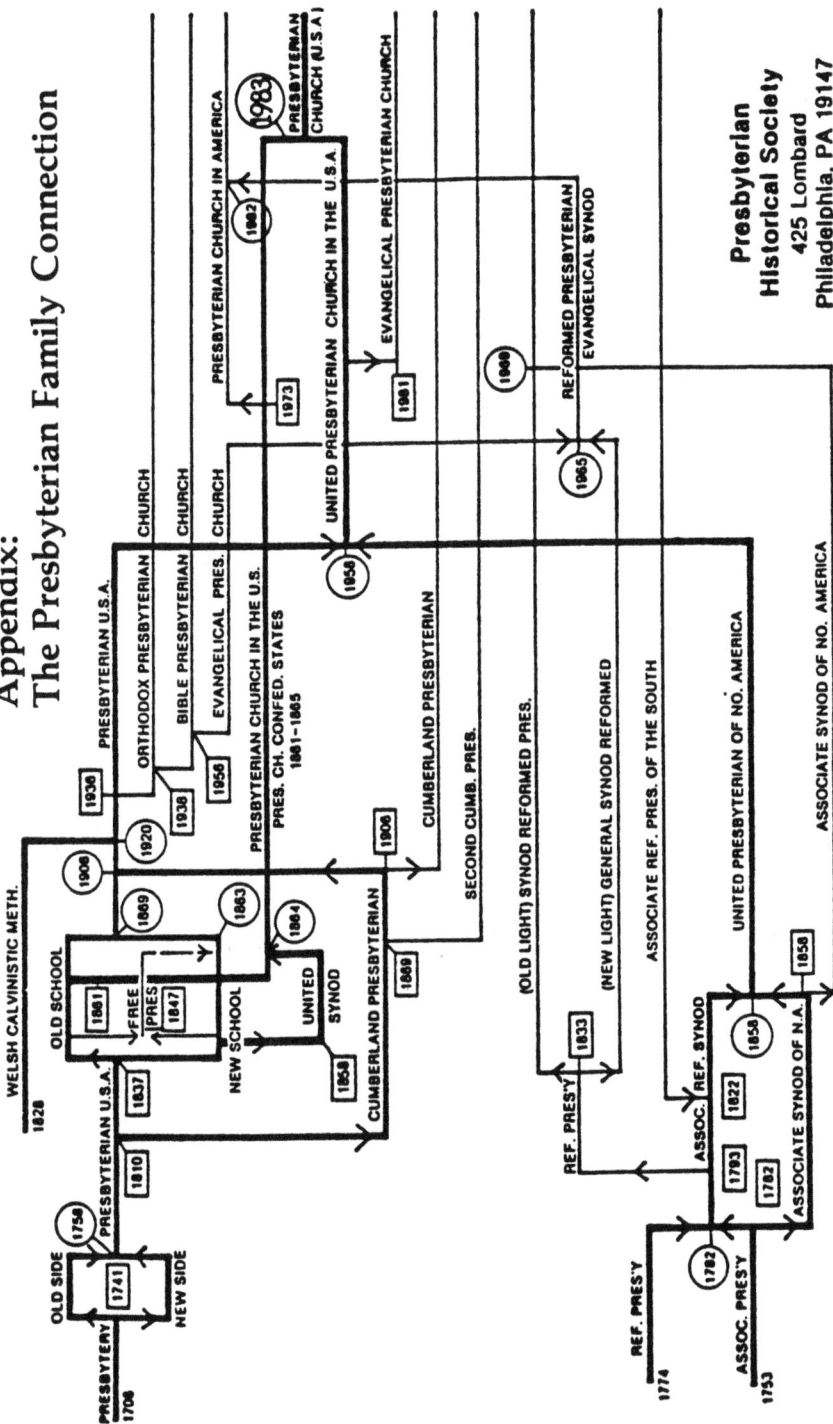

PRESBYTERIAN U.S.A.

WELSH CALVINISTIC METH. 1828

ORTHODOX PRESBYTERIAN CHURCH

BIBLE PRESBYTERIAN CHURCH

EVANGELICAL PRES. CHURCH

PRESBYTERIAN CHURCH IN AMERICA

PRESBYTERIAN CHURCH (U.S.A.)

UNITED PRESBYTERIAN CHURCH IN THE U.S.A.

EVANGELICAL PRESBYTERIAN CHURCH

REFORMED PRESBYTERIAN EVANGELICAL SYNOD

PRESBYTERIAN CHURCH IN THE U.S.
PRES. CH. CONFED. STATES 1861–1865

CUMBERLAND PRESBYTERIAN

SECOND CUMB. PRES.

(OLD LIGHT) SYNOD REFORMED PRES.

(NEW LIGHT) GENERAL SYNOD REFORMED

ASSOCIATE REF. PRES. OF THE SOUTH

UNITED PRESBYTERIAN OF NO. AMERICA

ASSOCIATE SYNOD OF NO. AMERICA

OLD SIDE

PRESBYTERY 1706

NEW SIDE

PRESBYTERIAN U.S.A.

OLD SCHOOL

FREE PRES

NEW SCHOOL

UNITED SYNOD

CUMBERLAND PRESBYTERIAN

REF. PRES'Y

ASSOC. REF. SYNOD

ASSOCIATE SYNOD OF N.A.

REF. PRES'Y 1774

ASSOC. PRES'Y 1753

1741 · 1756 · 1810 · 1837 · 1861 · 1847 · 1858 · 1864 · 1869 · 1863 · 1906 · 1908 · 1920 · 1938 · 1956 · 1936 · 1958 · 1965 · 1973 · 1961 · 1981 · 1982 · 1983 · 1833 · 1822 · 1858 · 1793 · 1782 · 1782

Unions 1756

Separations 1741

1706 First Presbytery
1717 First Synod
1789 General Assembly

Presbyterian
Historical Society
425 Lombard
Philadelphia, PA 19147

Index

Reference to specific collections is indicated by brackets, e.g., [ ]. For example, the citation, Aikin, Ruth [1], 4 refers to entry #1 on p. 4 of the text.

About the Author

FREDERICK J. HEUSER, JR., is an archivist for the Presbyterian Historical Society. He has contributed to *American Presbyterians: Journal of Presbyterian History*.

Presbyterian Historical Society Publications

Vol. I. *The Presbyterian Enterprise* by M. W. Armstrong L. A. Loetscher and C. A. Anderson (Westminster Press, 1956; Paperback reprinted for P.H.S., 1963 & 1976)

II. *Presbyterian Ministry in American Culture* by E. A. Smith (Westminster Press, 1962)

III. *Journals of Charles Beatty, 1762-1769,* edited by Guy S. Klett (Pennsylvania State University Press, 1962)

IV. *Hoosier Zion, The Presbyterian in Early Indiana* by L. C. Rudolph (Yale University Press, 1963)

V. *Presbyterianism in New York State* by Robert Hastings Nichols, edited and completed by James Hastings Nichols (Westminster Press, 1963)

VI. *Scots Breed and Susquehanna* by Hubertis M. Cummings (University of Pittsburgh Press, 1964)

VII. *Presbyterians and the Negro—A History* by Andrew E. Murray (Presbyterian Historical Society, 1966)

VIII. *A Bibliography of American Presbyterianism During the Colonial Period* by Leonard J. Trinterud (Presbyterian Historical Society, 1968)

IX. *George Bourne and "The Book and Slavery Irreconcilable"* by John W. Christie and Dwight L. Dumond (Historical Society of Delaware and Presbyterian Historical Society, 1969)

X. *The Skyline Synod: Presbyterianism in Colorado and Utah* by Andrew E. Murray (Synod of Colorado/Utah, 1977)

XI. *The Life and Writings of Francis Makemie,* edited by Boyd S. Schlenther (Presbyterian Historical Society, 1971)

XII. *A Younger Church in Search of Maturity: Presbyterianism in Brazil from 1910 to 1959* by Paul Pierson (Trinity University Press, 1974)

XIII. *Presbyterians in the South,* Vols. II and III, by Ernest Trice Thompson (John Knox Press, 1973)

XIV. *Ecumenical Testimony* by John McNeill and James H. Nichols (Westminster Press, 1974)

XV. *Iglesia Presbiteriana: A History of Presbyterians and Mexican Americans in the Southwest* by R. Douglas Brackenridge and Francisco O. García-Treto (Trinity University Press, 1974; 2nd edition, 1987)

XVI. *The Rise and Decline of Education for Black Presbyterians* by Inez M. Parker (Trinity University Press, 1977)

XVII. *Minutes of the Presbyterian Church in America, 1706-1788* edited by Guy S. Klett (Presbyterian Historical Society, 1977)

XVIII. *Eugene Carson Blake, Prophet with Portfolio* by R. Douglas Brackenridge (Seabury Press, 1978)

XIX. *Prisoners of Hope: A Search for Mission 1815-1822* by Marjorie Barnhart (Presbyterian Historical Society, 1980)

XX. *From Colonialism to World Community: The Church's Pilgrimage* by John Coventry Smith (Geneva Press, 1982)

XXI. *Facing the Enlightenment and Pietism: Archibald Alexander and the Founding of Princeton Theological Seminary* by Lefferts A. Loetscher (Greenwood Press, 1983)

XXII. *Presbyterian Women in America: Two Centuries of A Quest for Status* by Lois A. Boyd and R. Douglas Brackenridge (Greenwood Press, 1983)
XXIII. *Kentucky Presbyterians* by Louis B. Weeks (John Knox Press, 1983)
XXIV. *Merging Mission and Unity* by Donald Black (Geneva Press, 1986)
XXV. *Gilbert Tennent, Son of Thunder* by Milton J. Coalter, Jr. (Greenwood Press, 1986)

*Out of print

9 780313 262494